HORSE & PONY BOOK

CAROLYN HENDERSON

A DK PUBLISHING BOOK

LONDON, NEW YORK, MELBOURNE, MUNICH, AND DELHI

Editor Clare Lister
Designer Joanne Little
Jacket Design Neal Cobourne
Design Manager Jane Thomas
Category Publisher Sue Grabham
With thanks to the original team:
Project Editor Claire Bampton
Project Art Editor Lesley Betts
Photography Andy Crawford and John Henderson

First published in the United States in 2002
This paperback edition first published in 2007
by DK Publishing, 375 Hudson Street
New York, New York 10014

07 08 09 10 11 10 9 8 7 6 5 4 3 2 1
CD013 – 05/07

Color reproduction by Colourscan, Singapore
Printed and bound by Toppan, China

**Discover more at
www.dk.com**

Contents

Improve Your Riding Skills

Horse and Pony Care

Horse and Pony Breeds

Shows and Events

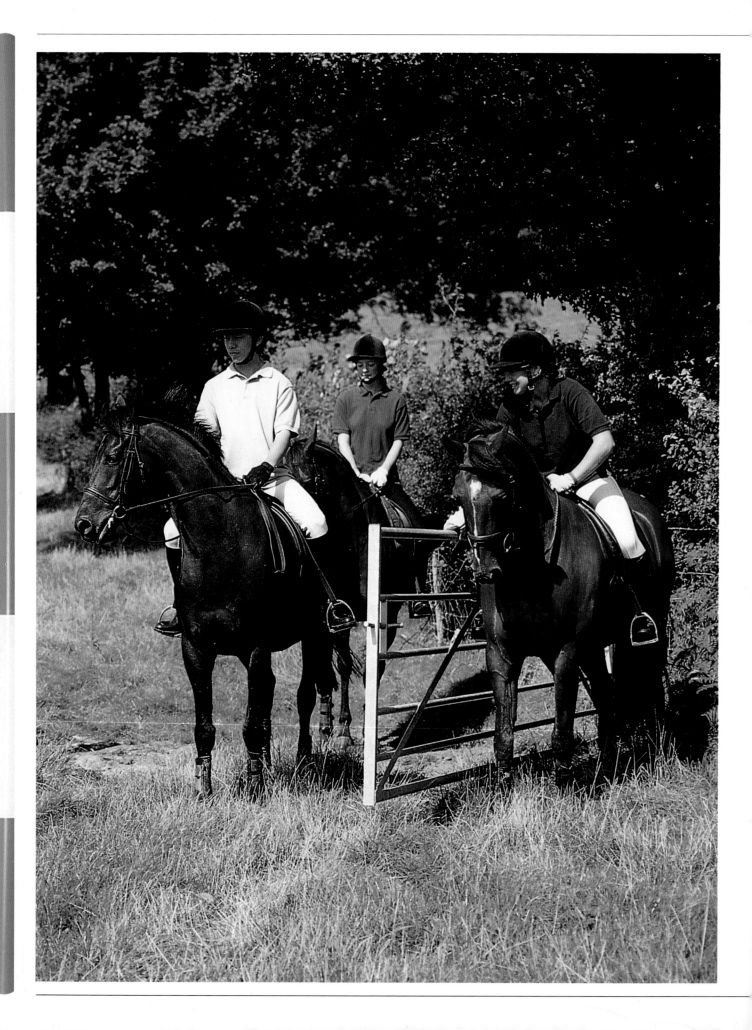

IMPROVE YOUR
RIDING
SKILLS

GETTING STARTED

THE BEST PLACE to learn to ride a pony is at a good riding stable. Here there are experienced trainers who have learned how to work with novice riders. These trainers are familiar with the most suitable horses and ponies on which to learn, so your lessons will be safe and enjoyable. Try to take a lesson at least once a week – more often if you have the chance.

Instructor leads pony while you ride.

Ready to ride

Dress safely and comfortably for your lessons. Always wear a hat or helmet that meets the highest safety standards. Many stables will lend you one at first, but eventually you will need to buy your own. Never buy a secondhand hat, since it may have been damaged in a fall. Jodhpurs or comfortable pants and riding boots or safe shoes are also essential.

Hat must fit properly.

YOUR TRAINER
During the first few lessons, your trainer will lead your pony using either a lead rein or a long lunge rein. This allows you to concentrate on sitting correctly and getting used to the feel of riding.

Always fasten the safety harness.

Horse should be in good condition – neither too fat nor too thin.

Tack should fit the horse well and be correctly adjusted.

Stirrup irons must be the correct size, so your feet cannot slide through or become trapped.

Long rubber riding boots or short jodhpur boots are suitable for beginners.

THE RIGHT PONY
Your trainer will choose a horse or pony for your lessons that is the right size for you. It should be quiet, friendly, and reliable and be used to being ridden and handled by beginners.

Horse should be well shod.

Choosing a riding stable

Friends who are also learning to ride may recommend suitable stables. Local vets, tack shop employees, and pony club officers may also have addresses of suitable establishments. Visit a stable before arranging for any lessons and check that it seems well run. Horses should be in good condition and the staff friendly and helpful.

THE STABLE

The grounds should be neat, with tools and equipment stored safely. There should be an enclosed riding arena. Some schools may also have indoor arenas.

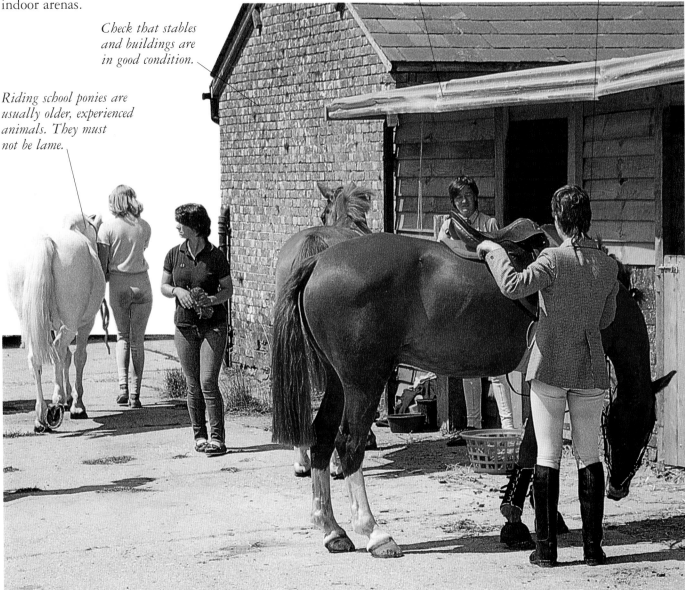

Ponies must have shelter from bad weather and shade from heat when tied up.

Trainer should check tack before rider mounts.

Check that stables and buildings are in good condition.

Riding school ponies are usually older, experienced animals. They must not be lame.

TACKING UP

TACK UP IN A STABLE, or outside with a halter fastened around the horse's neck so that you have control over it. Try to be gentle and quiet when you tack up, so that the horse remains calm. Make sure that the tack is safe and check it regularly for loose stitching or cracked leather.

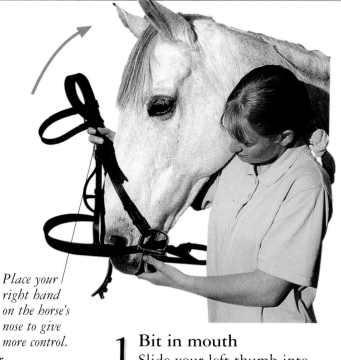

Place your right hand on the horse's nose to give more control.

Putting on a bridle

Before you start to put on a bridle, make sure the noseband and throatlatch are undone. Put the reins over the horse's head, remove the halter, and fasten it around the horse's neck to prevent it from walking away.

1 Bit in mouth
Slide your left thumb into the corner of the horse's mouth and gently guide the bit in.

Treat ears with care.

Check that the bit fits comfortably. If it is too low in the mouth, it could hit against the horse's teeth.

2 Over the ears
Put the headstall over the horse's ears and place the ears through the gap between the headstall and browband. Try not to pinch the ears. Take the forelock out from under the browband.

When you have buckled up the throatlatch, check that it fits correctly.

3 Fastening straps
Fasten the noseband and throatlatch. Once fastened, you should be able to fit a hand's width between the throatlatch and horse's face, and two fingers between the noseband and face.

Taking off a bridle

Before removing the bridle, make sure the horse is secure with a halter around its neck. Then unfasten the noseband and throatlatch, bring the reins to the poll, and slide the bridle and reins forward and off. Wait for the horse to release the bit from its mouth, or the bit may get caught or bang on its teeth.

Bring the reins to the poll.

Check that the noseband and throatlatch are undone.

Putting on a saddle

First check that the stirrup irons are run up, the saddle pad is in place, and the girth is folded over the saddle.

Girth folded over saddle.

1 In position
Lower the saddle gently over withers and slide back into position so coat hairs lie flat.

2 Fastening girth
Pull saddle pad up into the saddle. Carefully release girth so that it dangles down. Reach under the horse's belly for the girth, and fasten it. You should be able to slide your fingers between the girth and the horse.

Fasten one buckle at a time.

Taking off a saddle

Take off your saddle with as much care as you put it on. Once you remove the saddle, put it where it will not get damaged.

Place leathers between stirrups and saddle.

1 Run up stirrups
First run the stirrups up the leathers so they do not bang against the horse. Undo the girth.

2 Remove saddle
Place the girth over the saddle. The outside of the girth should be facing away from the saddle, so that any dried mud does not scratch it. Carefully lift off the saddle.

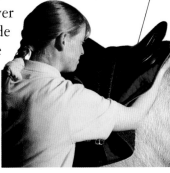

Lift saddle from horse's back.

Saddle must not pinch withers.

The stirrups should always be run up when you are not riding.

The girth should be tight enough to stop the saddle from sliding.

If leaving the horse tied up, twist reins under the throatlatch.

All tacked up

Once tacking up is finished, check all fastenings and see that the tack fits correctly. The bit should be high enough to fit snugly into the corners of the mouth. Straighten the bit, noseband, and browband if necessary. Tighten the girth, then gently pull each foreleg forward to release any wrinkled skin.

WELL-FITTED SADDLE
A horse can only work well if its tack fits and is comfortable. The tree, or frame, of a saddle must be the correct width. A properly fitted saddle will not pinch, rub, or interfere with the horse's movement.

MOUNTING AND DISMOUNTING

ONE OF THE FIRST things you learn when riding is how to get on and off a pony. One way to mount is to put one foot in the stirrup and to jump up. You can also mount by standing on a mounting block, or by asking for a leg up. There are also different ways to dismount.

Mounting

Before you begin, make sure the girth is tight enough to stop the saddle from sliding around. Most riders mount from the left side, facing the horse's tail.

Landing heavily may cause the pony discomfort.

Leg clears pony's back.

Keep reins short so that the pony does not move forward.

Stand with your left shoulder next to the pony's left shoulder.

2 Lowering into saddle
Swing your right leg over the pony's back, being careful not to kick the pony. Gently lower yourself into the saddle.

1 Foot in the stirrup
Turn the back edge of the stirrup toward you, place your left foot in it, and jump up off your right foot.

3 In the saddle
Slip your right foot into the stirrup. Take up a light feel on the reins and sit up tall. Check your girth before you ride off.

Sit straight in the saddle.

Dismounting

Get off with as much care and consideration as you used to get on. You may need to ask someone to help you if you are getting off a young or difficult pony.

Lean forward to start the swing down.

Keep reins short so that you are in control of the pony.

Try to avoid kicking or prodding the pony as you dismount.

Bend your knees as you land on the ground.

1 Start of dismount

Take both feet out of the stirrups, lean forward, and swing your right leg carefully over the pony's back.

Swing right leg over pony's back.

2 Jumping down

Let yourself down in a quiet, smooth jump without pulling the saddle over. Try to keep your balance as you land.

Alternative dismounting

Some riders keep one foot in the stirrup as they dismount. Take your right foot out of the stirrup and swing your leg over the horse's back. Keep your weight over the horse's withers. When your legs are parallel, slip your left foot from the stirrup and jump down to the ground. Always dismount in the way that your trainer tells you.

In Australia, riders dismount by keeping one foot in the stirrup.

IN THE SADDLE

LESSONS ON THE LUNGE or lead rein will get you used to the feel of sitting on a moving horse. Your trainer will help you achieve the correct position so that you and your horse are well balanced. You will also learn to give your horse clear instructions, called aids, with your legs, hands, and body weight. If you give the correct aids, and your horse is well trained, you will soon feel in control.

Hold the reins slightly apart, with your thumbs on top.

HOLDING THE REINS
Hold the reins in both hands, so that they pass between your little and ring fingers, through your palms, and out between your index fingers and thumbs.

Your first lesson

Your first lesson is usually on the lunge and may be spent mainly at the walk, though you may be able to try a few trotting strides. Your instructor will control the horse, so you can concentrate on your riding technique. Do not worry if there seems to be a lot to remember – it becomes easier with practice.

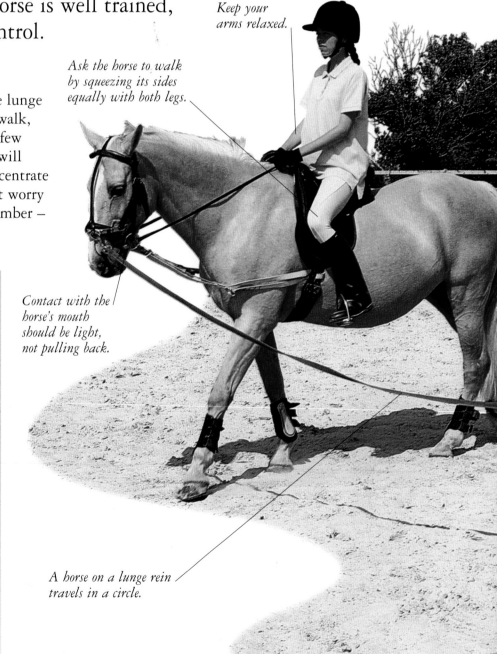

Keep your arms relaxed.

Ask the horse to walk by squeezing its sides equally with both legs.

Contact with the horse's mouth should be light, not pulling back.

A horse on a lunge rein travels in a circle.

FIRST LESSON

- Feel the horse's mouth without pulling on the reins

- Look ahead, not down

- There should be a straight (perpendicular) line through your shoulder, elbow, hip, and heel

- Think about absorbing the horse's movements through your lower back

- Think about sitting tall but staying supple

- Stirrups should stay under the widest part of your foot

Adjust the buckles one at a time.

A horse may expand its belly as you tighten the girth, so check it again after a few minutes.

TIGHTENING THE GIRTH

During one of your first lessons, you may be taught how to tighten the girth. To do this, hold the reins in your right hand and swing your left leg forward. Lift the saddle flap with your left hand and tighten the girth. You should be able to fit the flat of your fingers between the girth and the horse.

ADJUSTING STIRRUP LEATHERS

To adjust the stirrup leathers, hold the reins in one hand and pull the stirrup leather out and down, keeping your foot in the stirrup. Slide the buckle prong into the correct hole and pull the stirrup leather back up so the buckle is at the top again.

Keep your toes pointing forward and your heels down.

Keep your foot in the stirrup while you adjust the length of the stirrup leather.

Markers are used for more complicated exercises in later lessons.

The riding arena should be a safe, enclosed area.

The trainer controls your horse so you can concentrate on sitting correctly and getting used to the feel of a moving horse.

THE FIRST STEPS

WHEN YOU HAVE LEARNED how to sit on a horse at the walk, you will be ready to learn to control your horse's direction and speed by yourself. To communicate with a horse, give it signals with your legs, seat, hands, and voice. These are called the natural aids and will be used first of all to start, stop, and turn.

Voice

Hands

Sit tall, without bracing your back.

Seat

Reins should not be tight or hang in loops.

Legs

Starting off

Before moving off, check that your stirrups are the correct length and that your girth is tight enough. Your legs should rest lightly against the horse's sides and your reins should be at a length that gives a light contact with the horse's mouth, without pulling.

THE AIDS

The aids are signals that a horse is trained to understand. For example, a gentle squeeze of the legs means walk forward, and closing the fingers on the reins means stop. Stop giving the aid as soon as the horse obeys, or it will become confused.

Straight line from elbows through hands to horse's mouth

Feel the side-to-side movement in the seat.

1 Using the natural aids
Look ahead and close both legs gently against the horse's sides. Stop squeezing as soon as it walks forward. If there is no response, pause, then squeeze a little harder.

2 Starting the walk
Allow your hands to follow the movement of the horse's head, so contact with its mouth is light and flexible.

The Walk

The walk has a 1-2-3-4 rhythm. The sequence of steps is left hind, left fore, right hind, and finally right fore. The horse always has at least two feet on the ground at any one time. A horse naturally has a long walk stride and a relaxed neck.

Right hind leg is followed by right foreleg.

Try not to restrict the walk when riding the horse.

Artificial aids

Experienced riders may use equipment such as whips, spurs, and martingales to give signals. These are called artificial aids and must be used with care. Whips and spurs must never be used to hurt a horse and should not be used by beginners.

Martingale helps control head carriage.

Training whip reinforces leg aids.

Spurs must be blunt.

Sitting tall and still helps to slow down horse.

Ears back and relaxed means horse is paying attention to rider.

Horse should stay relaxed through neck and mouth.

Outside leg is behind the girth to stop horse's hindquarters from swinging out.

Wrists should be supple and straight.

3 **To stop the horse**
To halt, sit tall and tighten your seat and thigh muscles. Close your fingers on the reins without pulling back. Keep your legs in contact with the horse's sides to keep the horse balanced.

Halt should be square with legs together.

Turning

When turning, look where you want to go, so that you position your weight correctly. To turn left, squeeze gently on the left rein and also with the left leg. Allow the right rein to loosen slightly so the horse's head can turn. Don't try to turn sharply.

TROTTING

A HORSE HAS four gaits – walk, trot, canter, and gallop – and you will learn about each in turn. Trot can be ridden sitting, when the movement is absorbed through the rider's lower back, or rising, when the rider sits and rises in time with the horse's stride. Both become easier with practice.

Start by riding on the right diagonal.

Sit for one beat, then rise again to change diagonals.

Left hind foot and right forefoot touch down together.

DIAGONALS
Changing diagonals switches the position of the rider's weight. This makes riding easier for the horse, just like switching a heavy object from hand to hand makes it easier for you to carry. To change diagonals, sit for one beat, then rise again.

Learning to trot
Most riders spend more time in rising trot than in sitting trot. This is because as long as the rider is balanced and does not bump up and down, rising is more comfortable for the horse and easier for the rider. Western riders sit to a slow trot, called a jog.

Bend elbows slightly to maintain light rein contact.

1 Moving forward
To move forward from a walk to a rising trot, close your legs against the horse's side in a quick inward squeeze. Hold the reins to allow a light contact with the horse's mouth.

Close both legs on horse's side with a quick, inward nudge.

Walk should be active before asking for trot.

Legs move in diagonal pairs.

The trot

The trot is a two-time gait in which the legs move in diagonal pairs. The right (offside) foreleg and left (nearside) hind leg move forward at the same time in a 1-2, 1-2 rhythm. A trotting horse naturally moves in balance, with rhythmic strides.

Only one foreleg or hind leg bears the horse's weight at any one time.

Hock joints provide power to push horse forward.

Rise in a slightly forward, not upward, position.

2 Rising up into trot

Let the horse's stride push you slightly forward and out of the saddle. Do not grip with your knees or try to stand in the stirrups.

Horse's movement pushes you out of the saddle.

Move back into saddle as gently as possible.

3 Sitting down

Sink back into the saddle and let the horse's movement push you forward and out again. Counting the 1-2, 1-2 rhythm of the trot out loud might help.

Right foreleg and left hind leg move forward together.

Rider's knee and ankle joints absorbs her weight.

EXERCISES IN THE SADDLE

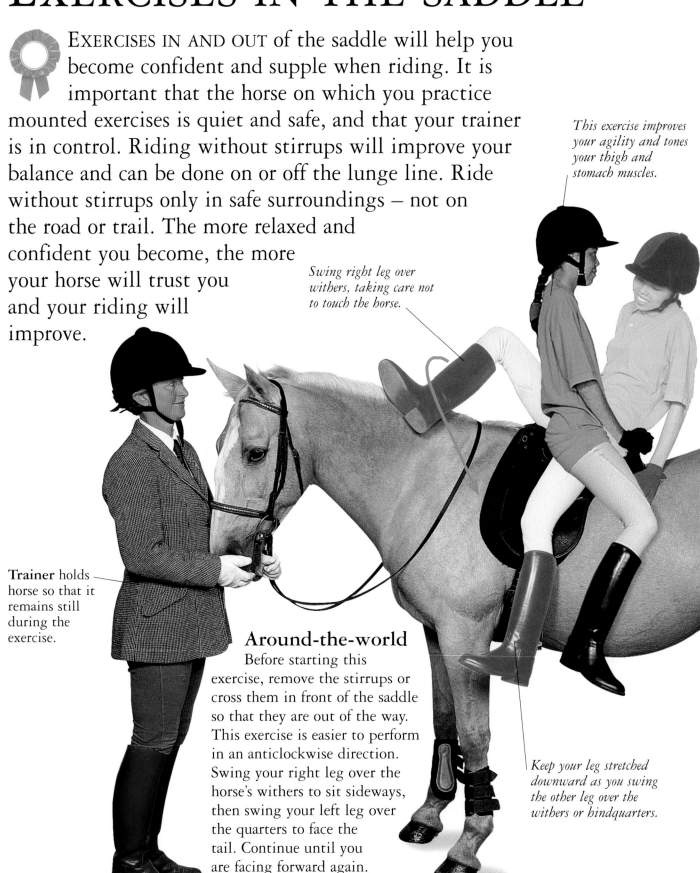

EXERCISES IN AND OUT of the saddle will help you become confident and supple when riding. It is important that the horse on which you practice mounted exercises is quiet and safe, and that your trainer is in control. Riding without stirrups will improve your balance and can be done on or off the lunge line. Ride without stirrups only in safe surroundings – not on the road or trail. The more relaxed and confident you become, the more your horse will trust you and your riding will improve.

This exercise improves your agility and tones your thigh and stomach muscles.

Swing right leg over withers, taking care not to touch the horse.

Trainer holds horse so that it remains still during the exercise.

Around-the-world
Before starting this exercise, remove the stirrups or cross them in front of the saddle so that they are out of the way. This exercise is easier to perform in an anticlockwise direction. Swing your right leg over the horse's withers to sit sideways, then swing your left leg over the quarters to face the tail. Continue until you are facing forward again.

Keep your leg stretched downward as you swing the other leg over the withers or hindquarters.

Without stirrups

Riding without stirrups is an excellent way to improve your balance and helps you absorb the horse's movement through your lower back. This exercise is especially good for improving your sitting trot. Start off by riding without stirrups for short periods, then rest.

Side reins control horse's head carriage when it is on the lunge.

Allow your legs to stretch down without gripping with your knees.

Forward stretch

This exercise helps you improve your balance. While walking, bend forward from the hip and stretch out your arms toward the horse's ears. Try to keep your lower leg in the correct position, without moving it too far forward or back.

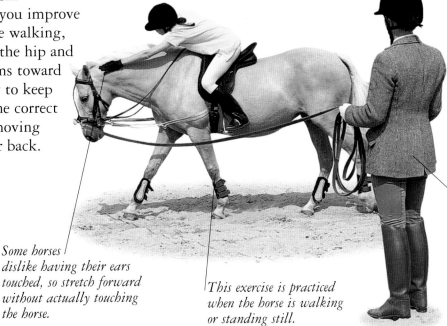

A moving horse must be controlled by a trainer.

Some horses dislike having their ears touched, so stretch forward without actually touching the horse.

This exercise is practiced when the horse is walking or standing still.

Getting in shape

There are lots of ways to improve your fitness and suppleness, even when you are unable to ride. Swimming is excellent for allover exercise and uses many of the muscles you use when riding. Biking and skipping are also beneficial for building leg muscles. Increase exercise times gradually or you may end up with aching muscles! Floor exercises such as the ones shown here may also help.

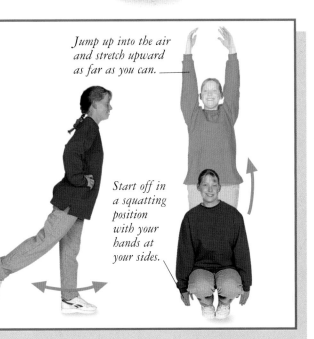

Jump up into the air and stretch upward as far as you can.

Start off in a squatting position with your hands at your sides.

Swing each leg forward and backward from the hip to loosen muscles.

CANTERING AND GALLOPING

THE CANTER AND THE GALLOP are faster than the trot. The gallop is the fastest gait of all and when galloping you must stay in complete control. During a gallop, bend forward from the hips so that your weight is just out of the saddle and is absorbed by your knees and ankles. During a canter, sit upright but remain relaxed, and absorb the horse's movement through your lower back.

Sit upright, but remain relaxed and look ahead.

Horse takes a longer stride with its right leg.

THE LEADING LEG
A cantering horse takes a longer stride with one foreleg than the other. This is called the leading leg. On a circle or bend, the correct leading leg is the inside leg – for example, in a clockwise circle, the right leg leads.

Preparing to canter
Before you ask a horse to canter, establish a balanced but active trot. It is easier to get the correct leading leg (also called the lead) by asking for a canter when you are trotting in a circle or in one corner of the arena.

1 Ask for canter
Maintain an active trot without rushing. Sit for one or two strides, then brush your outside leg slightly behind the horse's girth. At the same time nudge your inside leg near the horse's girth.

2 The canter
Try not to restrict the horse's head and neck as it moves into the canter. Sit tall but remain relaxed, and keep your lower back supple to absorb the movement.

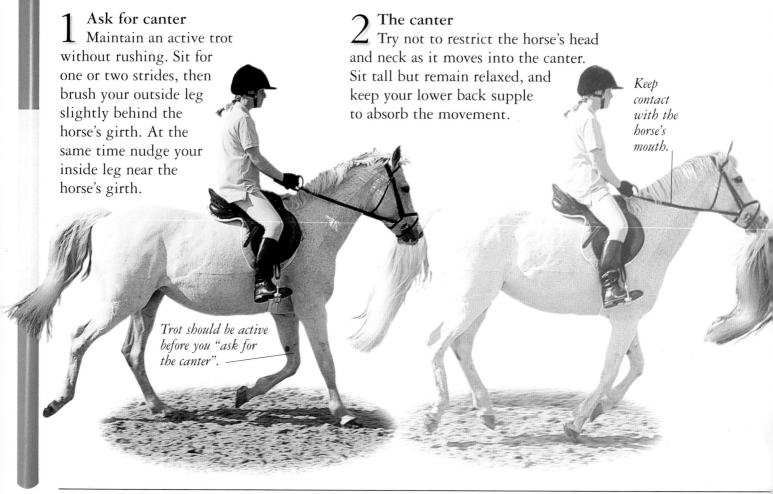

Trot should be active before you "ask for the canter".

Keep contact with the horse's mouth.

Galloping

Once you can canter properly, you can learn to gallop.
Instead of keeping your seat as you do for a canter,
bend forward from the hips and shift your weight just
out of the saddle. Only gallop in safe surroundings
where the visibility and terrain are good. You should
be in control of the pace, not the horse. The gallop has
a 1,2,3,4 four-beat gait.

Maintain a forward position.

Shorten stirrups by one or two holes to make it easier to stay balanced.

Cantering gait

A canter has a 1,2,3 three-beat gait.
When the horse's right leg leads, the left hind
foot falls first, then the right hind foot and the
left forefoot together, then the right forefoot.

Hindquarters provide power.

Horse's neck stretches as speed increases.

Use your weight distribution and the rein to give the horse a "slow down" signal.

3 Slowing down

To return to a trot, sit up
and tighten your thigh and
seat muscles. At the same
time, close your fingers on
the reins without
pulling back.

Changing pace is called making a transition.

4 Back to a trot

As the horse
moves into a trot,
relax your fingers on
the reins. Sit for one
stride, then move
forward into a
rising trot.

A trot is often more energetic just after the horse has cantered.

MAKING PROGRESS

YOUR FIRST LESSONS will be given to you one-on-one by a trainer, but as you gain confidence you will probably join a group lesson with other new riders. During the group lessons you will learn how to control your horse around other horses, and how to perform different exercises in the schooling arena. You will develop your knowledge of aids to communicate more effectively with your horse.

Right rein allows the horse to turn.

Left rein instructs the horse which direction to follow.

USING THE CORRECT AIDS
Your trainer will help you develop a more detailed knowledge of how to use the aids. For example, to turn left, look left, squeeze the left rein, and release the right rein slightly. At the same time, close your left leg on the horse's side and move your right leg back to control the angle of the hindquarters.

Group lessons
Your group will contain up to five or six riders. Riding in a group teaches you to be aware of other horses and their riders. Always keep a safe distance from the horse in front, since it might kick.

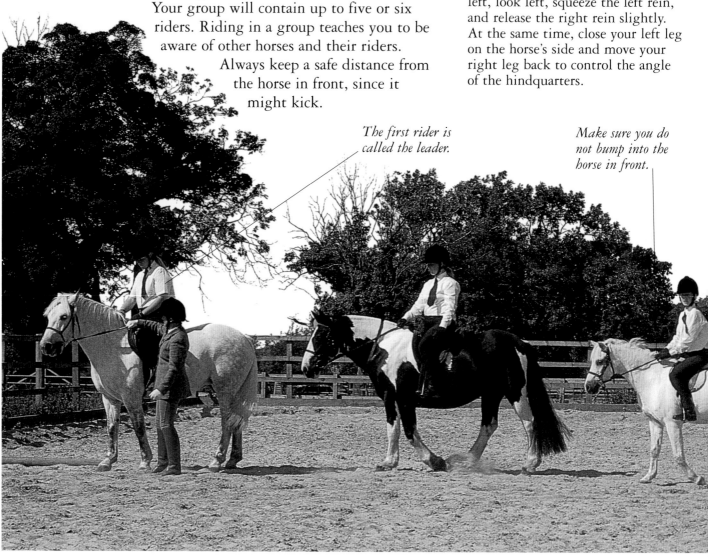

The first rider is called the leader.

Make sure you do not bump into the horse in front.

Passing side by side

When you pass another horse and rider, you need to make sure that you do not bump into them. The easiest way to do this is to pass so that your left hand is next to the other rider's left hand. This is called riding left hand to left hand.

Left hands are next to each other as you pass.

When passing a horse that you do not know, or that is unpredictable, allow enough space in case it kicks.

THE SCHOOLING ARENA

Most of your work takes place in the schooling arena. Letters placed around the outside of the arena are used as guides for starting and finishing circles and other exercises called school figures. A standard arena is $65^{1}/_{2}$ ft x 131 ft (20 m x 40 m).

SCHOOL FIGURES

THE STANDARD ARENA	CIRCLES	CHANGING THE REIN
This standard arena is ideal for schooling exercises.	*The small circle is 33 ft (10 m) in diameter.*	*The figure eight enables you to change direction.*

The letters around the arena are always A, K, E, H, C, M, B, and F. Markers D, X, and G are placed along the center of the arena.

You can ride 66-ft (20-m) circles in a walk, trot, and canter from A, C, B, or E. Advanced horses and riders ride in smaller circles.

Turning across the schooling arena to change direction is called changing the rein. In this case it is practiced across the diagonal.

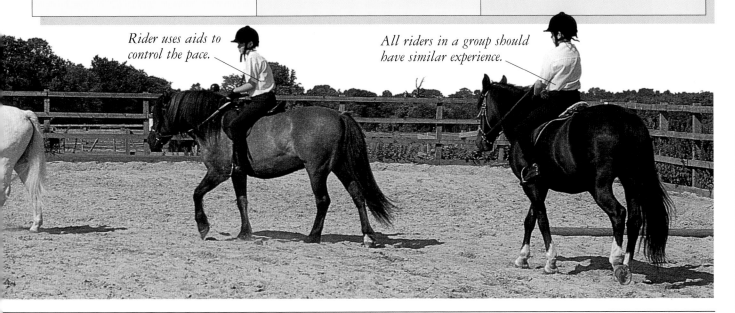

Rider uses aids to control the pace.

All riders in a group should have similar experience.

LEARNING TO JUMP

ONCE YOU CAN TROT and canter confidently, you can learn to jump. Before you start, you need to shorten your stirrups two or three holes so that you can stay in balance and follow your horse's movement. Always warm up before jumping so your horse is supple and obedient.

How a horse jumps

There are five phases to a jump – the approach, take-off, (suspension) in the air, landing, and departure. Keep your approach positive but calm, whether you are riding in trot or canter, and meet the fence straight. Look ahead and let your weight sink down to your heels.

Ground pole is at correct distance from fence for horse's stride length.

FIRST JUMP
Your first jump will be two poles in a low cross, approached from trot. A correctly placed pole on the ground in front, called a ground pole, helps you arrive at the correct takeoff point.

Knees act as shock absorbers.

Body weight should sink down through your legs into your heels.

Rider allows horse freedom of head and neck.

1 Takeoff
As the horse takes off, fold your upper body forward from the hips, and slide your hands far enough up the horse's neck to allow it freedom to stretch.

Horse pushes off with both back hooves.

Trotting poles encourage horse to flex hocks.

2 In the air
Think about sliding your seat backward as you fold; do not stand up in the stirrups. As the horse's head and neck stretch forward and down, give slightly with the reins.

TROTTING POLES
Poles spaced to allow one or more trot strides between them are called trotting poles. Use these to practice establishing a rhythmic stride and to introduce inexperienced horses to colored poles.

JUMPING PROBLEMS

If you are having problems, keep calm and go back to basics: perhaps your approach was hesitant or too fast. Never jump without a knowledgeable helper to advise you and alter fences. Always be ready to lower fences to make things easier and to restore the confidence of both you and your horse.

REFUSAL
A horse may stop in front of a fence or duck out to the side. This is called a refusal. A horse may refuse if the fence is too large or intimidating – if so adjust the fence. Ride straight at the fence with impulsion. You may have more control approaching at the trot.

CAT JUMP
A horse that jumps awkwardly instead of following a smooth arc through the air is said to cat jump. It usually happens when the horse takes off too close to the fence or is hesitant. To avoid this, try to establish a rhythm to the horse's strides and have impulsion.

Upper body becomes more upright.

Look up and ahead, either to your next fence or straight ahead if jumping a single fence.

Stirrup under widest part of foot

Light, unrestricting rein contact

3 Landing
As the horse lands, allow your upper body to become upright, without leaning back. Absorb landing impact through knees and ankles.

Horses should always wear protective boots.

Falling off
Everyone falls off occasionally, often because the horse or rider loses balance. Minimize the impact of falling by always wearing a hard hat or helmet and body protector. If you do fall, don't keep hold of the reins since the horse may step on you.

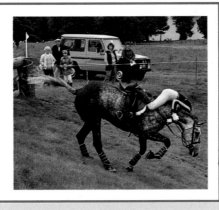

TRAIL RIDING

RIDING IN THE OPEN is called trail riding and is lots of fun. Horses enjoy trail rides and may be more lively than usual, so your trainer should make sure you are a confident, competent rider before taking you out. Most trail rides last for one or two hours and consist of a group of horses and riders. Before going on your first trail ride, make sure you know the rules of road safety, and that you have the right equipment.

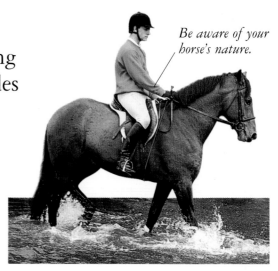

Be aware of your horse's nature.

TRAIL HAZARDS
During a trail ride, you may have to cope with potential hazards, such as riding through water. If your horse is reluctant or nervous, keep calm and allow a confident horse and rider to go first. Following another horse's lead gives an inexperienced horse confidence.

Out and about

Before you leave the stable, always tell someone where you are going and when you expect to be back. When out, respect rights-of-way and ride slowly past farm animals and people. Canter only when the ground is suitable and when you can see far enough ahead.

The most experienced rider should set a pace that everyone can keep up with.

Check the girth before riding out.

SAFE TRAIL RIDES

The correct preparations and equipment will enable you to trail ride in safety and with enjoyment. Only experienced horses should be taken out alone. Never take out a horse that is nervous in traffic. Ride out only when you are feeling confident.

CHECKING BEFORE RIDE

CHECK TACK
Before you set out, it is important to check that your tack is in good condition and correctly fitted to the horse. Make sure your girth is tight enough and that all straps are fastened properly, with any loose ends pushed through the securing loops. There should be no wrinkles or folds in pads or cloths used underneath the saddle.

TACKING UP

CHECK SHOES
Pick out the horse's hooves with a hoofpick and be sure that all four shoes are in good condition. If a shoe is loose, the horse should not be ridden until the farrier has replaced it.

SAFETY EQUIPMENT

FLUORESCENT CLOTHING
Wearing fluorescent, reflective clothing in bad weather makes you more visible to other road users, especially drivers. Safety equipment includes belts and vests for riders, leg bands for horses, and lights that clip onto the stirrup irons.

SAFETY GEAR

Fit leg bands on to horse.

Stirrup light

Place adjustable belt around your waist.

ROAD SAFETY

OBSERVATION
To ride out safely, be observant. Look ahead and behind before you move off, change direction, or pull out to move around parked cars or other hazards. At an intersection, stop and look in all directions, making sure it is safe before you proceed. Look ahead for things that may make your horse shy, such as roadwork, then check the road is free from traffic before riding past these obstacles. Never rely on your hearing – some cars are quiet and bicycles can't be heard. Stay on the side of the road, so other road users can pass you.

Remember to check behind as well as in front.

ROAD SENSE

HAND SIGNALS
Give hand signals before crossing roads or turning at intersections, and look both ahead and behind to make sure the road is clear before moving on. To turn right, hold your reins in your left hand and extend your right arm. To turn left, put the reins in your right hand and extend your left arm. Use the hand signals early enough and always ride on the same side as the traffic. Like motorists and cyclists, you must obey all road signs and traffic lights. Road users who don't realize they can frighten a horse will not warn you if they are near. Always thank drivers who slow down or wait.

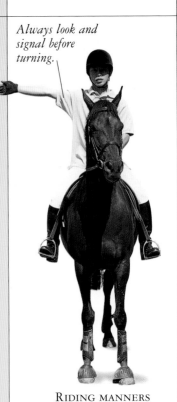

Always look and signal before turning.

RIDING MANNERS

ADVANCED RIDING

When you can ride confidently at all paces, you can learn more advanced movements. Your horse must already be trained to do these exercises, or it will not understand your aids. All the exercises shown here help make a horse more supple and balanced. They are useful for all forms of riding, as well as dressage.

HOW A HORSE TURNS ON THE FOREHAND
As the horse looks to the right, the right hind leg crosses in front of the left one. At the same time, the horse pivots on its right foreleg. The horse should not move forward or backward.

Turning in place

This exercise is useful when opening gates. It is also the first step in teaching a horse to move sideways. When the horse moves its hindquarters around its front end, it is called a turn on the forehand. At first, ask for just a few steps.

2 Move sideways
Hold your left leg on the girth and pull gently on the left rein to ask the horse to move sideways, not forward or backward.

Rider must sit straight and must not pull back on the reins.

1 Begin turn
To turn to the right, squeeze your fingers on the right rein and put your right leg back to nudge the horse behind the girth.

Right hind leg crosses over in front of left.

Don't practice this exercise too often or for too long.

3 Using legs
Use your right leg in time with the horse's steps, not as a constant push. Practice this exercise in both directions by using the opposite rein and leg aids.

Rein back

When your horse can rein back, it is easier for you to open gates and maneuver in tight spaces. You will need to start this exercise from halt. Close both legs behind the girth; at the same time, close your fingers on the reins and sit lightly to tell the horse to step backward, not forward. You can teach a horse to rein back by asking a helper to press gently on its chest as you give the aids.

Horse and rider are in position to move backward.

Rider maintains contact on reins.

Steps should be calm and even, and horse should move in a straight line.

LATERAL WORK

Exercises in which a horse moves sideways and forward at the same time are called lateral work. These make a horse more obedient and supple. If you go sideways at too steep an angle, your horse will stop going forward.

Rider's legs create energy.

Hands control energy and allow head and neck to stretch forward.

EXTENDED PACES

An advanced horse will be able to perform extended walk, trot, and canter. This is when the horse's strides are as long as possible, but are not rushed. The first stage in achieving extension is to practice riding lengthened strides down the long side of the arena or across the diagonal. The rider must stay in balance with the horse's movement.

Horse's legs cross over as it moves forward and sideways.

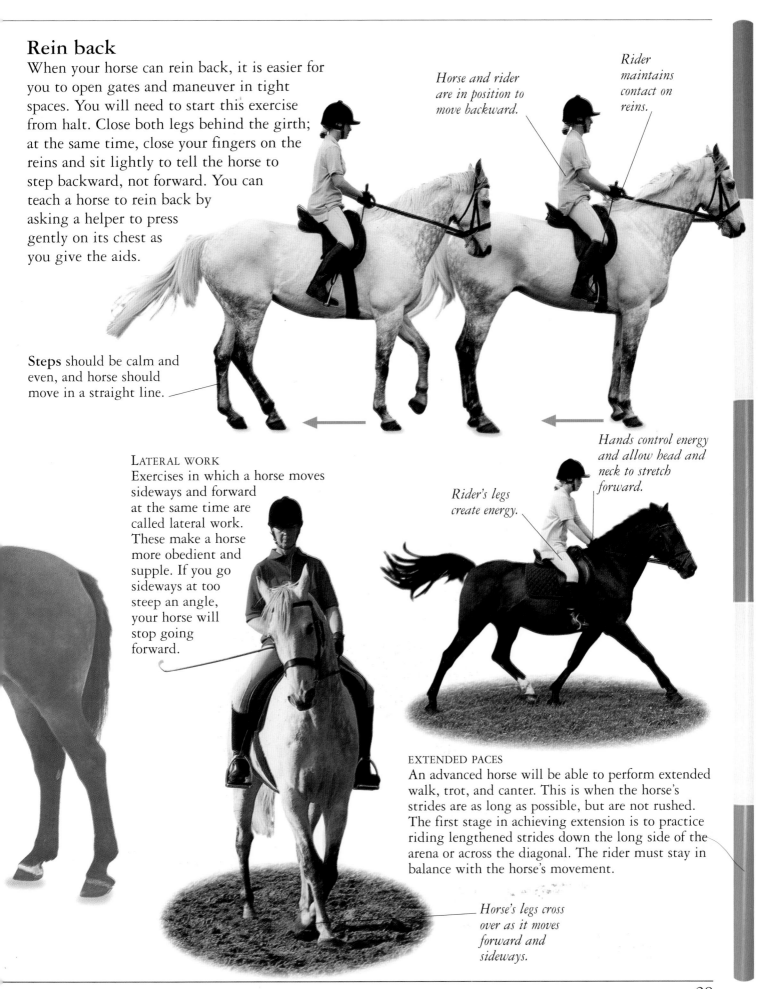

ADVANCED JUMPING

ONCE YOU HAVE MASTERED the basics of jumping, you can enjoy challenges such as jumping courses and tackling cross-country fences. To improve your ability, your trainer will set up jumping exercises in which a certain number of strides are allowed between each fence. This is called gridwork. Practice fences should be low. Never jump without having someone there to help.

CROSS-COUNTRY
Cross-country courses are ridden at a faster canter than show-jumping courses and are set over distances of about 1–3 miles (1.6–4.8 km). Some fences, such as drop fences and some water jumps, should be approached at a trot.

Jumping a course
A novice show-jumping course has about 10 fences. Approach each fence straight on at an energetic but controlled pace, and make sure your horse always canters on the correct lead. If necessary, jump from a trot.

Protective boots should be put on a horse when jumping to minimize the risk of injury.

Look up and ahead, not down at the fence.

Allow the horse to stretch its head and neck forward as it jumps.

WARMING UP
Warm up over a single fence before jumping a whole course. Start with a cross pole, which is easy for the horse.

Gridwork

A grid is a row of fences spaced at set distances to allow the horse to take a certain number of strides between them. It helps train the horse into meeting each fence correctly so that you can concentrate on riding correctly. More difficult grids improve a horse's athletic ability. Always get help to adjust the fences.

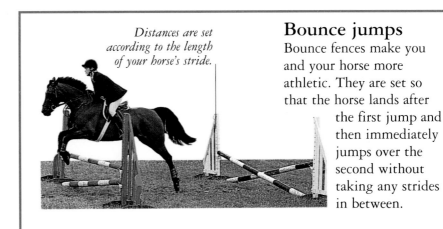

Distances are set according to the length of your horse's stride.

Bounce jumps

Bounce fences make you and your horse more athletic. They are set so that the horse lands after the first jump and then immediately jumps over the second without taking any strides in between.

The horse should jump the small cross pole and land at a canter.

A basic grid can be used for novice horses and riders, or for warming up.

The first pole, on the ground, should be approached at a trot.

The horse should take two strides in a canter between fences.

The second cross pole is the same height as the first.

JUMPING DISTANCES

Distances between the two fences of a double are set according to a horse's size and stride length, and the type of jump used. The higher and wider the jump, the more room is needed. This chart shows some distances used between upright and parallel fences.

ONE NONJUMPING STRIDE		
HORSE HEIGHTS			
	TWO UPRIGHT FENCES	AN UPRIGHT THEN PARALLEL	TWO PARALLELS
Over 14.2 hh	24ft–26ft (7.30m–7.90m)	23ft 6in–25ft (7.15m–7.60m)	23ft–24ft (7m–7.30m)
14.2 hh	21ft 6in–24ft 6in (6.55m–7.45m)	21ft 6in–23ft 6in (6.55m–7.15m)	Not used
13.2 hh	20ft 6in–23ft (6.25m–7m)	Not used	Not used

TWO NONJUMPING STRIDES		
HORSE HEIGHTS			
	TWO UPRIGHT FENCES	AN UPRIGHT THEN PARALLEL	TWO PARALLELS
Over 14.2 hh	34ft 6in–36ft (10.50m–10.95m)	34ft 6in–35ft 6in (10.50m–10.80m)	34ft–35ft (10.35m–10.65m)
14.2 hh	31ft 6in–35ft (9.60m–10.65m)	31ft 6in–33ft 6in (9.60m–10.20m)	31ft 6in–33ft 6in (9.60m–10.20m)
13.2 hh	30ft–33ft 6in (9.15m–10.20m)	30ft–32ft 6in (9.15m–9.90m)	30ft–32ft 6in (9.15m–9.90m)

WESTERN RIDING

RIDING WESTERN STYLE, for pleasure and competition, is popular throughout the world. Western riders usually prefer to use curb bits or bitless bridles called hackamores. The reins are held loosely in one hand, and the rider steers by leaning the rein against the horse's neck. This is called neck reining.

This rider is wearing casual Western clothes; show clothes have elaborate details.

Saddling up

Western riding equipment is different from English-style tack. The bridle has no noseband and it usually has a curb bit and split reins. The saddle has a high front and back, and the girth is called a cinch.

1 Put on bridle
Hold the bridle in front of the horse's face and slip the bit into its mouth. The split headstall (the top) goes around either side of the horse's ears.

The saddle blanket is made of heavy wool.

2 Put on the blanket
The saddle blanket helps absorb sweat and prevent rubbing. Place it on the horse's back. This horse is trained to stand still when the reins are dropped to the ground.

3 Put on the saddle
Position the saddle on the horse's back, move the left stirrup out of the way, then tighten the latigo (front) and cinch (girth) straps.

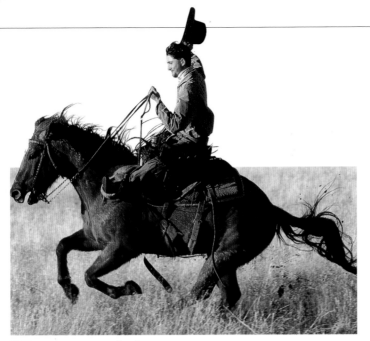

Western training

A highly trained Western horse will turn on the spot, move sideways, or make a sliding stop from a flat-out gallop in response to light aids. A horse can be trained so that it may be ridden in both English and Western styles.

Riders of the Camargue, in France, ride in a style similar to that of Western riders and use similar saddles. They are called gardiens, and ride white Camargue stallions to herd the region's wild black bulls. Like Western horses, these horses are also trained to change direction quickly.

The ficheroun is a three-pronged pole used to control bulls.

Crupper helps keep saddle in place.

Place stirrup iron over saddle.

Cinch strap

Food supplies are carried in the saddlebags.

Bedroll may have a waterproof cover.

Lariat for roping cattle is attached to the saddle horn.

4 Ready to go
A working cowboy's horse must carry all his equipment, including a bedroll.

TRAINING A HORSE

AN EXPERIENCED RIDER may be able to help train young or inexperienced horses. Training is enjoyable and rewarding, but must always be supervised by an expert. Practice skills such as long reining with an older, experienced horse before helping to teach a young one. Ride out a young horse in the company of a sensible horse and rider to boost the horse's confidence before taking it out alone.

Early lessons

Lunging and long reining teach a horse to obey voice commands. Long reining, where the trainer is positioned behind the horse, teaches it to stop, start, and turn and to accept the feel of a bit. This means that when a rider mounts the horse for the first time, the horse already understands some of the basic aids. Start by long reining in a safe, enclosed area.

USING LONG REINS
Long reins may frighten a horse when used for the first time. Before going outside, introduce the reins in the stable so that the horse is used to feeling them around its legs. When using the long reins, remember to use voice commands at the same time.

Gloves prevent injury if the reins are pulled through your hands.

Hard hat or helmet should always be worn when working young horses.

Riding boots are the safest footwear since they will not slip.

Long reins

Coil the long reins safely out of the way.

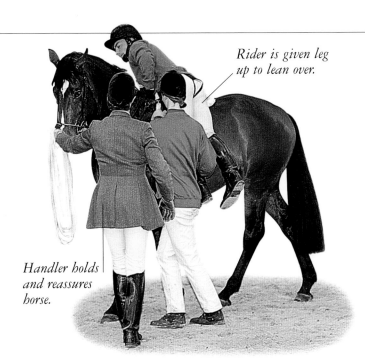

Rider is given leg up to lean over.

Handler holds and reassures horse.

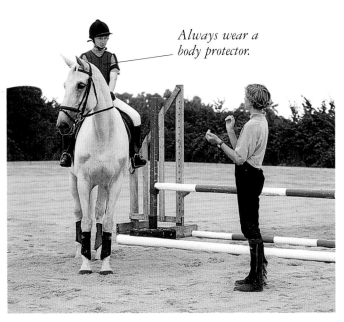

Always wear a body protector.

MOUNTING A YOUNG HORSE
Teaching a horse to accept a rider is challenging. First the rider leans over the saddle so that the horse gets used to the weight. When the horse is comfortable with the weight, the rider places one foot in the stirrup and swings the other leg over the saddle. Riding horses should not be ridden until they are three years old.

HELP FROM AN EXPERT
Introduce a horse to new skills, such as jumping, with expert help. A trainer will assess the horse's reaction to new experiences and decide when to progress to the next stage. Keep the first lessons short, and always finish on a good note so the horse stays relaxed.

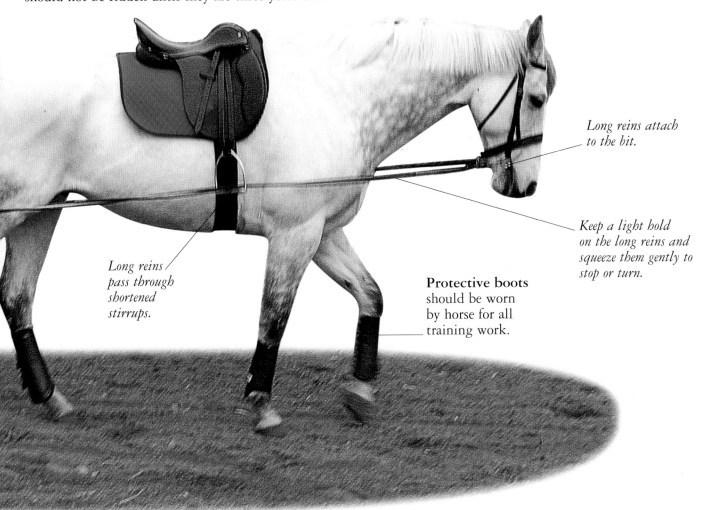

Long reins attach to the bit.

Keep a light hold on the long reins and squeeze them gently to stop or turn.

Long reins pass through shortened stirrups.

Protective boots should be worn by horse for all training work.

DIFFICULT PONIES

YOU MAY COME ACROSS PONIES that are difficult to ride or handle and that have specific behavioral problems. Never try to solve these problems alone – get help from an experienced adult. The expert should always start by checking that the pony is not uncomfortable or in pain, since this causes many problems. Ask your vet's advice if necessary, and get an expert to check the fit of your tack. Too much high-energy food and too little exercise will cause hyperactive or bad behavior.

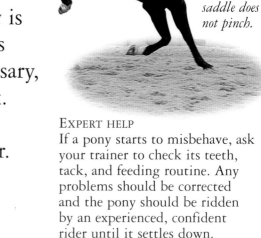

An experienced rider will not be thrown off the pony.

Check that saddle does not pinch.

EXPERT HELP
If a pony starts to misbehave, ask your trainer to check its teeth, tack, and feeding routine. Any problems should be corrected and the pony should be ridden by an experienced, confident rider until it settles down.

Difficult temperaments

Healthy ponies that have been trained and handled correctly should be confident and friendly. Ponies that have had rushed or incorrect training sessions, or those that have had bad experiences, may be nervous or stubborn. Naturally aggressive ponies are rare, but some may bite or kick to prevent you from doing something they dislike.

Male horses and ponies, called stallions, may rear up onto their hind legs to fight, and they may use their teeth and forelegs.

When a pony's ears are laid back it is confused or frightened.

AGGRESSIVE PONIES
Horses and ponies are sometimes aggressive with each other, but rarely attack people. Some kick or bite if previous rough handling has caused them pain. Do not try to separate ponies that are fighting in the field since you may get hurt.

NERVOUS PONIES
A pony may be generally nervous, or worried about particular things, such as traffic. It must be handled in a quiet and confident manner and ridden by an expert. Never go for a trail ride on a traffic-shy pony. It must be retrained by an experienced professional.

COMMON PROBLEMS

All ponies misbehave occasionally and even the quietest ones may buck, rear, shy, or bolt if startled. Problems occur when bad behavior becomes a habit. An out-of-control pony is too dangerous for anyone but an expert to deal with.

RIDING PROBLEMS

BOLTING
A bolting pony runs off in a panic, and ignores its rider's signals to stop. Never ride a pony that is known to bolt. If a pony gallops off when you are already riding it, slow down by pulling and slackening the reins repeatedly; do not pull the reins continuously. Use your voice to reassure the pony.

SHYING
A shying pony may jump sideways if something frightens it. If you spot something that your pony might shy at, turn its head slightly away from the hazard, and look ahead as you ride past. Use your legs to keep a pony moving and try not to tense up since the pony will sense that you are nervous.

A REARING PONY

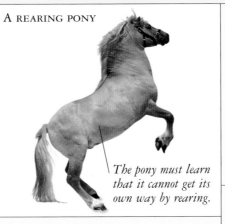

The pony must learn that it cannot get its own way by rearing.

REARING
If a pony rears while you are riding, lean forward and do not pull back on the reins. If you do, the pony may fall over backward. As the pony brings its feet back to the ground, ride forward with determination.

PULLING
If a pony pulls, have its teeth checked and make sure that its bit fits correctly. Get expert advice to find out if you need to use a different bit or noseband. Practice riding between a walk and a trot in the riding arena, using your voice as well as other aids. While doing this, give and take on the reins – don't just pull on them.

DIFFICULT TO MOUNT
If a pony is difficult to mount, ask someone to stand at the pony's head and hold the bridle. Use a mounting block instead of mounting from the ground, so there is no chance of the saddle being pulled over. Be careful not to dig your toe into a pony's ribs as you get on.

HANDLING PROBLEMS

PULLS WHEN LED
If your pony pulls, practice leading it in an enclosed area and make sure it understands your voice commands. Use a bridle, or a training halter that applies pressure when a pony pulls, and slackens when it stops pulling. When leading, pull and then slacken the reins or halter; do not pull constantly.

A pony should come when you show it food.

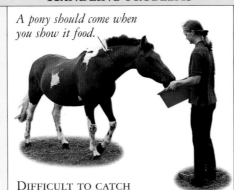

DIFFICULT TO CATCH

RUSHES OUT OF THE STABLE
Make sure the stable doorway is not too narrow – if a pony has banged against it at some time, it may rush out through fear. Use a bridle or training halter to give you more control. Reward a pony for good behavior, and practice until it has gained confidence.

DIFFICULT TO LOAD
The trailer must be light and inviting, with a safe, stable ramp. Allow plenty of time to practice when loading. Put protective leg wraps on the pony and wear a hat, safe boots, and gloves yourself. Some ponies gain confidence from following an experienced one. Don't give up!

DIFFICULT TO CATCH
Leave a leather or safety halter on a pony that is difficult to catch. Reward it with food when it comes to you. Catch the pony regularly, reward it, and then release it immediately so it does not think that coming to you always means work. Catch other ponies first, so that the pony has no friends left in the field.

KICKING
Never stand directly behind a pony, whether it kicks or not. If a pony is prone to kicking, try to find out why it kicks. Problems are often caused when girths are tightened too roughly. If this is not the case and it still kicks, speak sharply to the pony. Keep ponies that kick other ponies at a safe distance when being ridden.

FIRST AID AND SAFETY

TO RIDE SAFELY means preparing well, choosing the right clothes and equipment, and knowing what to do in an emergency. Always check that the pony's shoes and tack are in good condition, and never use damaged equipment. Learn the basics of first aid for both horses and people. This will help you to stay calm in an emergency when others may need your help.

Bag containing essentials can be fastened around the rider's waist.

FIRST-AID KIT
One rider in a group should carry a basic first-aid kit. This should include a hoofpick in case a pony gets a stone lodged in its hoof. If available, take a cell phone – switched off – for emergencies.

Riding out safely
Before leaving the stable always tell someone where you are going and when you will be back. If you are riding a pony for the first time, go out with a friend whose pony is quiet and reliable. Take trail rides in daylight only, and do not gallop on verges or pedestrian rights of way.

Hat cover is made from fluorescent, reflective material

Tack should be in good condition, particularly stitching on the reins, girths, and stirrup leathers.

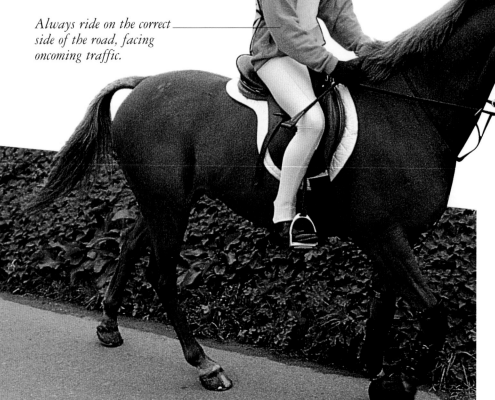

Always ride on the correct side of the road, facing oncoming traffic.

BEING SEEN
Make sure that other road users can see you from as far away as possible, so that they have a chance to slow down and pass safely. Wear fluorescent, reflective clothing, such as vests and hat covers, on overcast or rainy days. This is a sensible precaution to take in all weather conditions on busy roads.

Keep calm and reassure the rider, then have someone call emergency services.

Emergency first aid

If you witness a riding accident, try to prevent an injured rider from getting up. If the rider is unconscious, check his or her breathing and clear the air passages if necessary. Do not remove the rider's hat – a possible neck or back injury may be made worse. If the rider seems dazed or confused, he or she may have a concussion. Place the rider in the recovery position and call for help.

The recovery position is the safest position in which to place an injured person.

Stay with the injured rider until emergency services arrive.

Do not attempt to remove boots.

Cover the rider with a blanket if he or she feels cold.

Attending to horse injury

You may need to attend to an injured horse when you are out for a ride. If a fracture is suspected, keep the horse still and call the vet immediately. If blood is spurting from a wound, a main artery has probably been severed. Apply a clean pressure pad to minimize bleeding and call the vet.

1 Dress the wound
Gently clip hair from the edges of the wound and wash away any dirt with clean water. Place a sterile, nonstick dressing with padding over the wound.

Place padding over the dressing before using a bandage.

2 Secure the padding
Keep the padding in place with a self-adhesive bandage. Keep pressure even, but do not pull the bandage too tight.

Start at the top to secure padding, then move down to wound area.

Hold the leg firmly with one hand.

3 Finish up
Bandage the leg so that you leave an edge of padding at the top and bottom. Change the dressings twice a day to prevent the wound from becoming infected.

HORSE & PONY CARE

CONFORMATION, COLORS, AND MARKINGS

TO DESCRIBE OR ASSESS A HORSE, look at its conformation, coat color, and any markings. Good conformation, or shape, means that the horse has correct proportions. Different breeds and types have different characteristics, but the guidelines for good conformation are always the same.

Points of a Horse

The points of the horse are names given to parts of its head, body, and legs. They are like reference points on a map. Some parts have unusual names, such as the withers, so many people find it useful to learn all the points of a horse.

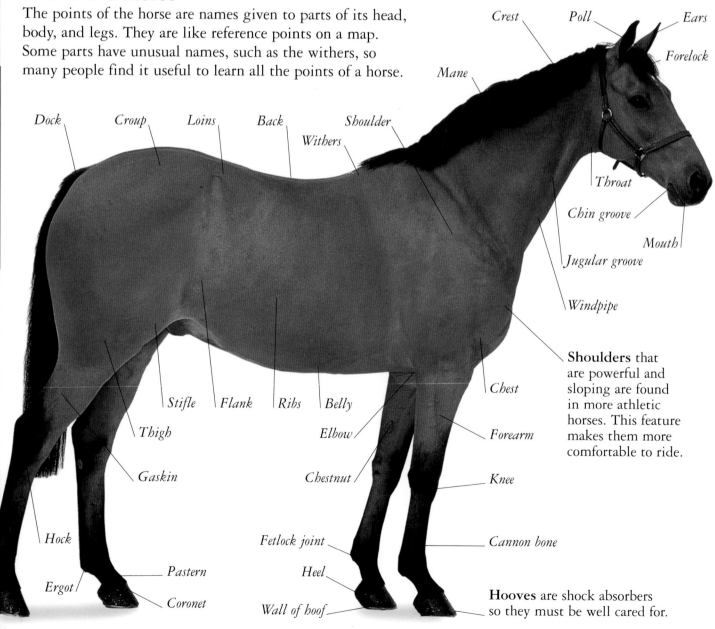

Crest Poll Ears Forelock Mane Throat Chin groove Mouth Jugular groove Windpipe

Dock Croup Loins Back Shoulder Withers

Shoulders that are powerful and sloping are found in more athletic horses. This feature makes them more comfortable to ride.

Chest Forearm Knee Cannon bone

Stifle Flank Ribs Belly Elbow Chestnut

Thigh Gaskin Hock

Fetlock joint Heel

Ergot Pastern Coronet Wall of hoof

Hooves are shock absorbers so they must be well cared for.

CONFORMATION

A HORSE'S CONFORMATION
Good conformation means more than good looks. It allows a horse to stand up to hard work because there is less strain on its body and legs. Judging conformation takes practice, but in general a horse's body should look symmetrical. Although all horses have strong and weak points, ideally the strong points compensate for the weak ones.

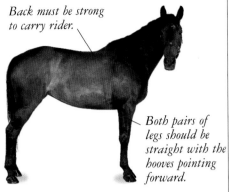

Back must be strong to carry rider.

Both pairs of legs should be straight with the hooves pointing forward.

Front legs take most of the strain during galloping and jumping.

Powerful hocks are the horse's engine.

BASIC COLORS

BASIC COAT COLORS
Coat colors are either solid or spotted. Color is often used to describe a horse. It does not affect a horse's performance, but many people have preferences. Some breeds, such as the Cleveland Bay and Palomino, are almost always the same color – Clevelands are bay and Palominos are gold. Appaloosas have spotted coats in varied patterns, such as blanket and snowflake. Gray horses vary from white to dark gray and can be plain, dappled, or "flea-bitten."

CHESTNUT

GRAY

BAY

DUN

PALOMINO

PAINT

FACE MARKINGS

FACE MARKINGS
Natural patterns of white hair on a horse's face range from those covering the forehead and front of the face to small snips around the mouth. Some horses have more than one face marking, such as a star and snip.

STRIPE   STAR   BLAZE   SNIP

LEG MARKINGS

LEG MARKINGS
Leg markings are usually white. If they come to below the knee or hock they are called socks. If they extend further up the leg they are known as stockings. Black spots on white hair around the coronet are called ermine markings. Hooves can be black, white, or black with white stripes.

White legs usually have pink, sensitive skin.

A white hoof accompanies legs with socks or stockings.

Black markings on a white coronet are called ermines.

STOCKING   SOCK   ERMINE

CARING FOR A HORSE OR PONY

LOOKING AFTER A HORSE OR PONY is a big responsibility. A pony needs someone to provide food, shelter, and water, and to keep it fit and healthy. As you spend time cleaning out the stable and grooming a pony, you will learn more about its habits and body language and will be able to assess how it is feeling. Taking care of a pony involves hard work throughout the year, but building a relationship with a pony can be very rewarding.

CHOOSE A PONY CAREFULLY
Try to spend time with different horses and ponies. This will help you avoid making mistakes when deciding which type would suit you best.

Treat a pony gently as if it is a friend. Loud noises may frighten it.

Ears pointing forward show that the pony is interested and happy with its surroundings.

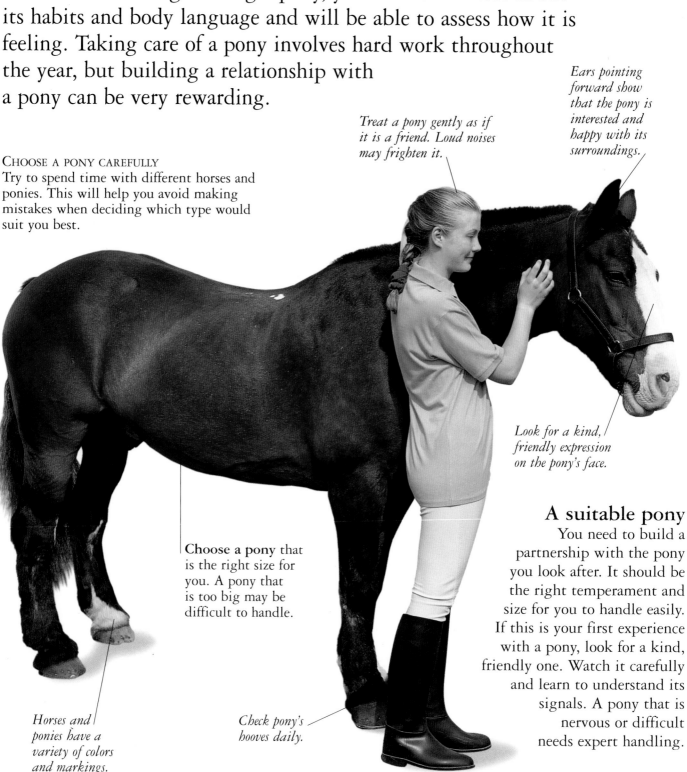

Look for a kind, friendly expression on the pony's face.

Choose a pony that is the right size for you. A pony that is too big may be difficult to handle.

Horses and ponies have a variety of colors and markings.

Check pony's hooves daily.

A suitable pony
You need to build a partnership with the pony you look after. It should be the right temperament and size for you to handle easily. If this is your first experience with a pony, look for a kind, friendly one. Watch it carefully and learn to understand its signals. A pony that is nervous or difficult needs expert handling.

Many young riders start by helping out at a riding school.

Helping out

One of the best ways of learning how to look after a pony is to help at a local riding stable. You can learn how to clean stalls, and groom and handle different types of horses and ponies, with experienced people to help you. Spending time at a riding school will help you decide whether you enjoy the commitment before you own or share a pony.

Grooming kit

Every horse or pony should have its own grooming kit. Wash the brushes regularly and rinse them thoroughly to keep them clean. Do not use one pony's brushes on another, or you might spread skin infections. A pasture-kept pony does not need much grooming as it needs to retain grease in its coat to protect it from the cold and rain. A stabled pony should be groomed more thoroughly.

Cleaning out

Stables should be cleaned out every day. A four-pronged fork is useful for lifting dirty straw bedding. For cleaning out a shavings bed, use a shavings fork. This allows clean bits of shavings to fall through the gaps, while catching any wet material and droppings. Some tools for cleaning out can also be used to remove droppings from fields. Remember to put your tools away when you have finished with them.

Hoof dressing

Body brush

Metal curry comb

Plastic curry comb

Mane and tail combs

Sweat scraper

Hoof pick

Sponges for the eyes, mouth, and nose, and another for the dock

Cloth

Rubber curry comb

Dandy brush

Yard broom

Shovel for picking up small bits of dirty bedding

Wheelbarrow for collecting manure

Waterproof boots

Shavings fork

Rake for raking gravel yard

Pitchfork, sometimes used for putting down straw bed

Straw fork

Small rake and skip for picking up manure

HANDLING A HORSE

HORSES AND PONIES respond best to quiet, confident handling. Keep movements smooth, and be gentle but positive when you touch a horse. Horses are bothered by sudden movements and loud noises; use your voice in a soothing tone to calm and speak sharply, but not loudly, to reprimand.

Be careful not to flip the halter over the horse's head and startle it.

The halter should be fastened securely but not too tightly.

Catching a horse

Take your time when trying to catch a horse. Even if you are in a hurry, try to give the impression that you have plenty of time. It is a good idea to occasionally catch a horse, reward it, then let it go, so it does not always associate being caught with being ridden.

2 Putting on haltering
Slip the lead rope round the horse's neck and put the halter over its nose. Pass the strap behind its ears and fasten.

1 Approaching the horse
Approach the horse from one side at a slight angle, so that it can see you. Stay relaxed so that your body language invites the horse to come toward you.

Keep halter low and still as you approach.

Allow the horse to smell you. You may also want to reward the horse with a treat, so that it is willing to be caught.

Turning a horse out

Open the gate wide enough for easy access and shut it before you let the horse go. Before releasing the horse, turn its head toward the gate, so that you do not get kicked by its hind legs if it gallops off.

Body language

Watch horses in the field to study their body language. Ears pointing back warn others to stay away. Groups of horses determine their own positions of authority, from the leaders to followers.

Flattened ears show tension.

How to tie a quick-release knot

When tying up a horse, tie the lead rope to a string loop so that if the horse panics the string will break. A quick-release knot is also used to tie up haynets.

1 Start of knot
Loop rope through ring. Bring the loose end around and across so that you have made a slanting figure eight.

This end of the rope attaches to the halter.

2 Making the knot
Pass the loose end behind both thicknesses of rope and then back through the bottom loop of your figure eight.

Keep loops big so that the rope passes through easily.

3 Secure the knot
Push the loose end back through the loop to make another one. Pull down on the loop you have just made to tighten the knot.

This is a secure but safe quick-release knot.

4 To undo the knot
To undo the knot, pull on the loose end of the rope. This knot allows you to release a panicking horse quickly and safely.

Pull on loose end.

TYING UP A HORSE
When tying up a horse, allow enough length of rope for it to move its head. Some may pull back if they are tied up too short.

Tie lead rope to piece of string for safety.

OUT IN THE FIELD

ALL HORSES AND PONIES should be turned out daily to graze and relax. Some can live out permanently, while others need stabling part of the time. Ponies that have had laminitis should not be turned out on rich spring grass or they may get it again. Horses need fields with safe fencing and gates, clean water, shelter and other horses for company. A field must be large enough to supply all the horses within it enough grass on which to graze and space to roam.

FENCES AND GATES
Gates should be properly balanced and easy to open and close when leading horses through. There are many safe types of fencing, such as post and rail. Never use barbed wire or your horse may injure itself. Check fencing for breaks every day.

The ideal field

An individual horse needs at least 1 acre (2 hectares) of land on which to graze. Try to graze your horse on grass that has been grown especially for horses – cattle pasture may be too rich. Shelter to protect a horse from wind and rain, and to shade it in summer, can be provided by trees and hedges, or a field shelter. Get expert advice on pasture management, such as fertilizing and resting land.

Poisonous plants

Check the pasture regularly for poisonous plants. Ragwort is particularly dangerous. It has yellow flowers and should be pulled up and burned immediately – this will help to stop them growing again. Yew, acorns, and deadly nightshade are also dangerous when eaten. Call your vet if you suspect a horse has been poisoned.

Acorn attached to oak leaf.

Yew leaves

Post and rail fencing is safe and strong. Replace broken or weak rails immediately.

If possible use a pasture where someone can keep an eye on the horses.

Grass should be weed free.

FRESH WATER

There must always be plenty of clean, fresh water. Use a special water trough or a safe container with no sharp edges. Keep the trough clean and free from things that could contaminate the water, and from ice in winter.

Horses will go thirsty rather than drink dirty or contaminated water.

Water trough should not have sharp edges since these could injure horse.

PASTURE MANAGEMENT

• Field must have safe fencing

• There must be a permanent supply of clean, fresh water

• Remove manure from field as often as possible

• Do not turn out ponies susceptible to laminitis on rich grass

• In winter, give hay in the field and, if necessary, extra feed

Field shelters must have openings large enough to allow more than one horse to go through at a time. If your field slopes, put your shelter on the highest point so rain drains away from the site.

Fresh drinking water is supplied in a trough.

Trees and thick hedging provide year-round protection.

Lighting to help see on dark winter nights.

CARE OF A PONY AT PASTURE

PONIES LIVING OUTDOORS in a field need daily care and attention. They have special needs at different times of year. For example, they need protection from insects in summer and from cold weather in winter. Check a pasture pony for injury or illness, and make sure that shelter and clean water are always available and the fencing is safe.

Security measures

Freeze marking is a security system that can help trace a stolen pony. The mark is frozen onto the pony's skin but does not hurt. Each freeze mark is unique. Other systems of identification are hoof branding, identichipping, and lip tattooing.

Horse is identified by the number.

ONI5

Checking the pony

Go and look over the pony at least once every day. A healthy pony is alert and not shivering. Make sure there are no signs of injury or illness and that its shoes and feet are in good condition. Look out for cuts and any signs of heat or swelling – small cuts may be hidden by a thick coat. Some ponies have pink skin around their noses that may get sunburned in the summer, so use some protective cream.

Leather halters or ones with a breakable safety insert should be used. If these get caught up, they are pulled off without injuring the pony.

Base of ears should be warm.

Hooves should be picked out daily.

Seasonal needs

A pony that lives outdoors needs different kinds of protection at different times of year. It is important that shelter is available all year round to give shade in the summer and protection from wind and rain in the winter.

A waterproof blanket can help give protection in the winter.

SUMMER NEEDS
Insects are the biggest problem in the summer. Some bite and can cause allergic reactions. Insect repellent helps to control them. You can also use a fly fringe, fastened to a halter, which helps to keep insects away from the pony's eyes.

WINTER NEEDS
Outdoor blankets protect the pony from cold, wind, and rain. Check that they fit correctly and don't rub. Have two blankets in case one gets torn.

Fly fringe protects pony's eyes from flies.

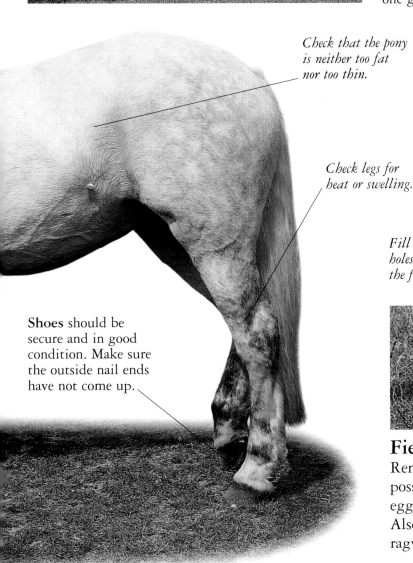

Check that the pony is neither too fat nor too thin.

Check legs for heat or swelling.

Removing manure regularly from the field is essential to protect a pony's health.

Fork through manure you can't pick up.

Fill in any holes in the field.

Shoes should be secure and in good condition. Make sure the outside nail ends have not come up.

Field care

Remove manure from the field as often as possible. This helps reduce the amount of worm eggs on the field and protect the pony's health. Also, pull up any poisonous plants, such as ragwort, and take them away to be destroyed.

THE STABLE

THE IDEAL STABLE is designed so that the horses are healthy, happy, and safe and so that the design is convenient for people using the stable. There may be outdoor stables or stables inside a large building called an indoor barn. Feed, hay, and bedding should be stored near the stables, but not so close as to be a fire risk. The stable must be built with safety and security precautions.

INDOOR BARN
Indoor barns allow you to clean out and groom out of bad weather. They must have wide central walkways for tying up and leading out horses, and good ventilation and drainage. There should be large doors at each end, which should be left open when possible. Fire precautions are vital inside barns.

Stall design
Stalls must be light and large enough for a horse to walk around comfortably. Mares with foals need extra large stalls. Good ventilation and drainage are important for a horse's health. Ideally there will be windows at the front and back and ventilation at roof height. Pitched roofs provide more air space, and are therefore preferable to flat roofs.

Pitched roof gives more room for air to circulate.

Gutter must be kept clear of falling leaves and other blockages.

Burglar alarm for security

Special lights are covered for safety.

Gate should be shut to prevent horses escaping from stable.

Keep storage spaces clean to avoid attracting mice and rats.

Fire extinguishers should be easily seen and ready to use. Ask local fire-fighters for fire prevention advice.

Bedding materials

Wheat straw is a popular choice for bedding, but it contains a small amount of dust, which makes some horses cough. Paper, wood shavings, hemp, and rubber mats are alternative choices.

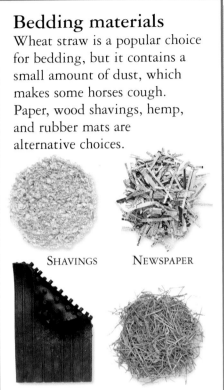

SHAVINGS   NEWSPAPER

RUBBER MAT   STRAW

Roof vents help keep air clean and healthy.

Manure heap should be kept tidy.

Cleaning tools should be stored neatly.

Top half of stable door is always left open to help air it out.

Cleaning out

Cleaning a stable must be done every day. Clean out completely if you use straw. Shavings, paper, and hemp are more absorbent, so remove manure daily and do a full clean out once or twice a week. If you can, take the horse out of the stable before you begin.

Dirty bedding is heavy, so only lift a little at a time.

1 Remove dirty straw

To clean out a straw bed, use a four-pronged fork to remove manure and wet, dirty straw. Separate out the clean bedding, then shovel up the dirty bedding into a wheelbarrow.

2 Brushing up

Sift through the remaining straw with your fork to check that it is clean. Pile it up round the sides and brush the floor thoroughly. Try to sprinkle some disinfectant on the bare floor once a week.

Add fresh bedding, piling it higher around the edges.

3 Laying down a bed

Fork piled up straw into the center of the floor and check that the sides of the stable are clean. Pile fresh straw high around the sides of the stable wall to give added protection to the horse.

THE STABLED PONY

KEEPING A HORSE or pony in a stable allows you to control what it eats and enables you to keep it clean and healthy. However, looking after a stabled horse or pony takes a lot of time and work and requires you to follow a strict routine. All stabled horses and ponies should be turned out for at least part of the day to keep them happy and relaxed.

Stable manners

Ponies must be taught to behave well so they are safe to handle in the confined space of a stable. Teach them to step back or move away from you when you apply gentle pressure and use voice commands.

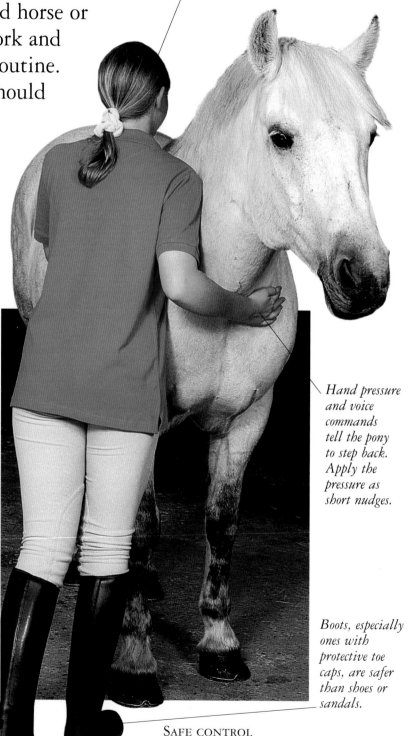

Use your voice firmly but quietly. Some ponies will respond to your voice commands alone.

Hand pressure and voice commands tell the pony to step back. Apply the pressure as short nudges.

Boots, especially ones with protective toe caps, are safer than shoes or sandals.

SAFE CONTROL
Your pony should be happy to obey your commands in the stable. It is important to allow your pony some times of peace and quiet, such as during feed times.

Anti-weave grid helps to stop pony from weaving over the door.

STABLE VICES
Ponies who do not like being confined may develop behavioral problems, or stable vices. These include swaying their heads from side to side, called weaving, or biting the stable door, called crib-biting. Ponies with stable vices may be happier when turned out to pasture.

DAILY ROUTINE

Ponies need a routine to remain healthy and happy. This means feeding them at the same time each day and giving them daily exercise. The combined system can be used where a pony is put out to pasture during the day and kept in a stall at night.

TIME	STABLE KEPT PONY	TIME	COMBINED SYSTEM
7:00 AM	Check for any signs of illness or injury. Adjust blankets if necessary and give fresh water and first feed.	7:00 AM	Check pony for illness or injury. Feed and leave to eat in peace. When finished, pick out hooves, put on outdoor blanket if not riding, and turn out. Check water supply and fencing, and give hay in field if necessary. Clean out.
7:45 AM	Tie up pony outside stall and clean out. Pick out hooves, remove blankets, and brush over. Exercise now or at a time that suits you, allowing one hour after pony has been fed.	8:00 AM	Brush over and exercise. If pony has been turned out, allow half an hour after bringing in. Make sure pony is cool on return from exercise, brush over or wash down, and check hooves. Fit blanket if necessary and turn out. *Make sure the blanket is fitted securely.*
9:15 AM	Tack up and ride out or train. Walk for the last 15 minutes of exercise to allow pony to cool down. Brush over or wash if sweaty, then put on outdoor blanket if weather is bad. Check hooves and shoes and turn out. Wash mangers and buckets.		
12:00 PM	Bring in and fully groom. Put on stable blankets. Give second feed and hay and check water. *Put hay in hay net and hang in stable.*		
		4:00 PM	Bring in pony and check for signs of injury. Pick out hooves and check shoes. Brush over, change blankets if necessary, and give hay. If wet, use breathable blanket that will transfer moisture away from body. Check one hour later and again if necessary. Change blankets so pony is dry and comfortable for the night.
2:00 PM	Check water, give more hay if necessary. Remove manure from stall (pick out).		
5:00 PM	Pick out and check water. Add or change blankets if necessary; remember temperature may drop at night. Give third feed and hay.	5:00 PM	Check that pony is dry and warm enough. Give second feed and check water.
7:00 – 10:00 PM	Pick out and check water and blankets. Give fourth feed, if required, and more hay. *The stable must be clean for the night.*	7:00 – 9:00 PM	Make sure pony is comfortable. Pick out and check water. Give hay and third feed if necessary.

FOOD AND FEEDING

HORSES NATURALLY EAT GRASS and hay, which is called forage. Forage must be of good quality since it is the main part of a horse's diet. When horses have a lot of exercise, they may need extra feed such as a grain mix or other supplement. Small, frequent meals are better for a horse's digestive system than large ones. Make sure clean water is always available. Allow one hour after feeding before you ride.

Feed your horse small amounts often.

The right amount

A horse needs between 1.5 and 2.5 percent of its bodyweight in food each day. For example a 660 lbs (300 kg) pony would need about 16.5 lbs (7.5 kg) food every day. Forage (grass and hay) should provide at least half, and usually more, of the total amount. If a horse is being worked hard, you may need to increase its feed in line with its work. Ask an expert if you are unsure of how much to feed.

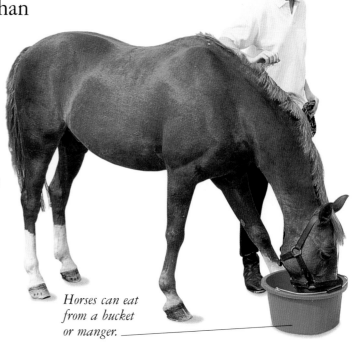

Horses can eat from a bucket or manger.

Feeding hay

Hay can be fed on the ground, in a haynet, or in a rack. Soaking hay in clean water helps prevent coughing. If soaking hay, submerge for up to one hour. Never feed a horse dusty or moldy hay.

1 Filling haynet
To fill a haynet, hold the top open with one hand and put hay in with the other. Be careful the string around the hay bale doesn't get tangled with the hay.

Shake hay to remove dust.

Pull net to correct height.

2 Placing haynet
Pass haynet drawstring through tie ring and pull the net up. This prevents the horse from getting its foot caught in an empty haynet.

WHAT TO FEED

Feed pellets or a grain mix (compound feeds), or cereals, such as oats. Compound feeds are best since they are specially formulated; don't add cereals, since they will alter the compound formula.

DIFFERENT FEEDS

MAIN FOODS
Oats and barley are traditional horse feeds. Flaked corn is fed only in small amounts to horses that are working hard. Bran should not be fed routinely – only feed it as a bran mash on your vet's advice. Sugar beet cubes are a good energy source but must be soaked in water for at least 12 hours before feeding.

GRAIN MIX

BARLEY

FLAKED CORN

CUBES

BRAN

OATS

SOAKED SUGAR BEET

SUPPLEMENTS

EXTRAS
All horses should have salt licks available. Horses also enjoy fruit and vegetables, especially carrots and apples, sliced and added to their feed. Some horses may need vitamin and mineral supplements or extras such as cod-liver oil. Always get expert advice before feeding these, since compound feeds already contain the vitamins and minerals a horse needs.

FRUIT AND VEGETABLES

Apple

COD-LIVER OIL

Rutabaga

Carrot

SALT LICK

VITAMIN SUPPLEMENT

3 Tying up haynet
Take the end of the drawstring down to the bottom of the haynet and pass it through one of the holes, about two thirds of the way down the haynet. Pull the net up again.

Pass loose end through the knot so it can't be pulled loose.

Pull up net to tie ring.

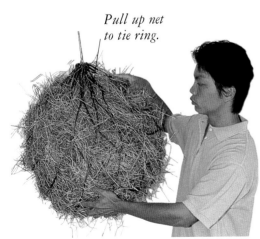

4 Fasten knot
Pass the loose end of the drawstring behind the other piece and pull it through in a loop. Pull down with both hands to make a slip knot that is secure but easy to undo.

How to weigh a horse
To calculate a horse's approximate weight use a weigh tape, which measures a horse's girth. This gives corresponding weights to measurements and enables you to decide how much to feed your horse.

Check horse's weight every two weeks.

GROOMING

DAILY GROOMING helps keep a pony clean and its coat, skin, and hooves healthy. Grooming also helps you get to know a pony and to check for any problems, such as heat in the legs, that may occur. A grooming kit contains special tools that are used for different purposes; keep brushes clean and only use them on the horse they belong to.

Use hoof pick from heel to toe.

PICKING OUT HOOVES
Use a hoof pick to clean a pony's hooves daily. Work downward, from heel to toe, and do not dig into the V-shaped frog.

Use the hand nearest the horse's body to groom, since it is easier to to put your weight into the brush strokes.

Tie the pony up outside, so that dust from grooming doesn't affect its breathing.

How to groom
Begin grooming by loosening the dirt in the coat with a rubber currycomb or groomer. Use a dandy brush to flick off loose mud. Using short strokes, remove oil with a body brush. Brush the mane and tail with a body brush or an ordinary hairbrush to avoid breaking the hair. Finally clean the eyes, nose, and dock.

1 Brushing pony over
Before riding out, brush your pony over and pick out its feet. Make sure that there is no dirt or dried mud on parts of the pony where tack or blankets will rest, since this might irritate. Check for mud on the back and girth areas, behind the elbows, the face, and the base of the ears.

USING A CURRYCOMB
To clean the body brush scrape it against a metal currycomb, then knock out the dust from the currycomb. Never use metal currycombs on a horse.

2 Cleaning eyes, nose, and dock
Use separate sponges, or pieces of cotton wool, to clean the eyes, nose, and dock. Dampen the sponges or cotton wool, then gently wipe the necessary parts of the pony. If your pony has a runny nose or weeping eye there may be a problem, so ask an expert for advice.

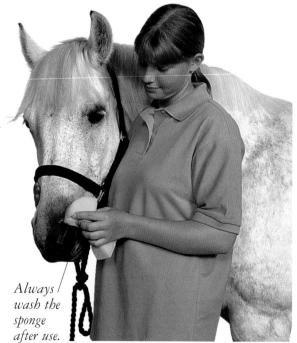

Always wash the sponge after use.

Care of a pasture-kept pony

Ponies that live outside need the natural oils in their coats to protect them from cold and wet. Before you ride a pasture-kept pony, remove dried mud with a rubber currycomb, then brush over with a dandy or whisk brush. Do not use a body brush on the pony's coat since it takes out the oils; only use a body brush to tidy the mane and tail. Finally pick out the hooves, and clean eyes, nose, and dock.

Thick coat has natural grease, which protects against wind and rain.

Bathing a pony

Only bathe a pony on a warm day. Wet the coat, then work the shampoo into the horse's coat with a sponge or shampoo glove. Rinse thoroughly, then repeat if necessary. Once finished, walk pony around until it is dry.

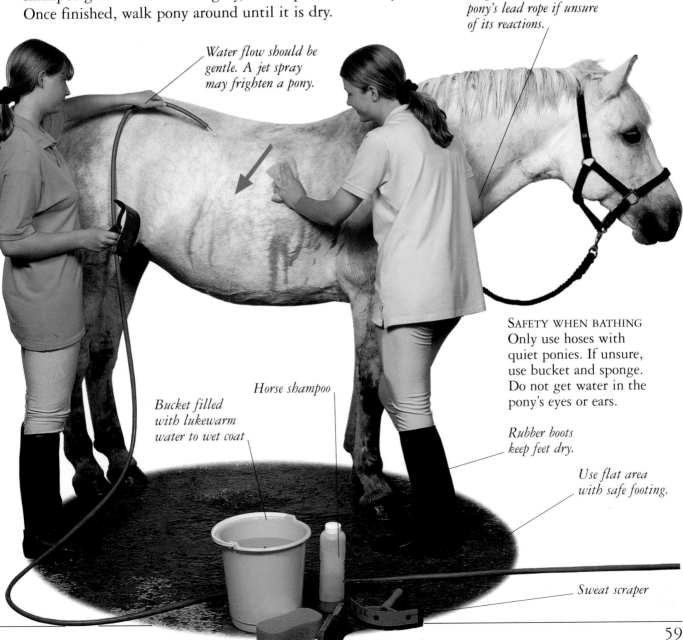

Water flow should be gentle. A jet spray may frighten a pony.

Helper should hold onto pony's lead rope if unsure of its reactions.

SAFETY WHEN BATHING
Only use hoses with quiet ponies. If unsure, use bucket and sponge. Do not get water in the pony's eyes or ears.

Rubber boots keep feet dry.

Use flat area with safe footing.

Horse shampoo

Bucket filled with lukewarm water to wet coat

Sweat scraper

MANES AND TAILS

SOME HORSES, such as Thoroughbreds, have manes and tails with fine hair. Others, such as mountain and moorland ponies, have thick ones that provide protection in bad weather. Manes and tails may be shortened and thinned by pulling out hairs. This makes horses look neater, and makes it easier to braid manes.

Ponies with coarse coats also have thick manes and tails.

NATURAL MANES
Outdoor ponies need the protection of a thick mane and tail against cold and dampness. The forelock – the part of the mane that falls between the ears – protects against flies.

Braids should be evenly spaced and the same size.

Whiskers act as feelers, so leave them if you prefer.

Plaits enhance shape of horse's neck.

A neat horse
Some people pull manes so they are easy to braid for competition; the tail should also be shortened to the correct length. Others may also trim whiskers and excess hair from ears, face, and legs. Some breeds, such as Arabians and mountain and moorland ponies, are shown with natural manes and tails that are not pulled or braided.

Pull the mane when horse is warm so hair comes out easily.

A well-groomed horse ready for competition

Fetlock and coronet hair is trimmed to give a neat outline.

Pulling a mane
To pull a mane, use a comb with short, narrowly spaced teeth. Back comb the top hair out of the way and take hold of four or five underneath hairs. Pull these out with a sharp, downward tug.

Trimming a tail

It takes two people to trim a tail – one to hold out the tail at the angle it is carried when the horse moves, the other to cut. Cut straight across the bottom at the correct length. The top of a full tail – one that has not been pulled – can be braided.

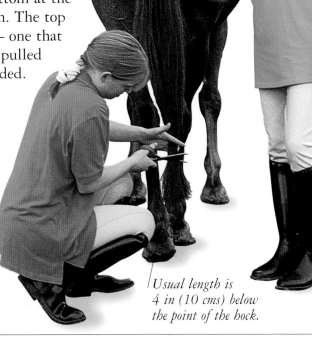

Pull quickly downwards.

Usual length is 4 in (10 cms) below the point of the hock.

PULLING A TAIL
Tail pulling creates a neat shape but some horses object to it. Stand to the side and pull three or four underneath hairs at a time from each side until you reach halfway down the dock (tail bones). If the horse is unhappy, stop or you may get kicked.

Avoid pulling front tail hairs – hair will stick up as it grows.

Tail end should be level when horse is on the move.

Putting on a tail bandage

A tail bandage encourages the hair of a pulled tail to lie flat. It also protects the tail hair from being rubbed out when traveling in a trailer.

Start with bandage rolled so tapes are on the inside.

1 From the top
Start at the top and bandage down to the end of the tail bone. Keep pressure firm and even, but not too tight.

2 Tying up
Wrap tapes around, tie in a bow at the front, and tuck in ends. Bend the tail gently into its normal position.

Tapes should be fastened no tighter than the bandage.

HOOVES AND SHOEING

A HORSE'S HOOVES, or feet, bear a lot of weight and help cushion the impact when a horse runs or jumps. In the wild, horses' hooves wear down naturally as they roam large distances, however domesticated horses need their hooves trimmed regularly by a farrier. Most working horses need metal shoes to protect their hooves on hard surfaces.

Rubbery frog absorbs jolts when hoof hits the ground.

Bar

Parts of the hoof

The hoof is a hard outer shell that encases sensitive structures such as bones, blood vessels, and cartilage. The bottom part is made up of the sole and a V-shaped wedge called the frog.

The front hooves should be almost round.

Sole

Toe

Hard wall

FOOT CONFORMATION
Good foot conformation is when the front and hind hooves each form a pair that are the same size and shape.

Regular trimming keeps the hoof in shape and prevents splits.

UNDERSIDE OF THE HOOF
The sole should be slightly concave rather than flat to help the horse grip the ground. The V-shaped frog acts as a pump for the hoof's blood supply.

How to check a horse's hooves

Check your horse's shoes and pick out its hooves once a day. Unpleasant smells, other than normal stable smells, are a sign of infection.

2 Get horse to pick up hoof
Squeeze the fetlock and use your voice to encourage the horse to pick up its hoof.

Keep your hand on the inside, not the outside of the horse's leg.

Make sure the horse is standing square before picking up a hoof.

1 Check the leg
Stand to one side, and run your hand down the leg checking for abnormalities.

3 Hold the hoof
As the horse lifts its hoof, catch the toe. Do not lift the leg too high.

Try not to hold the hoof up for long periods.

Dressing the hoof

Cosmetic hoof dressings give a shiny appearance to the hoof. They are used after grooming, for special occasions such as shows. Do not use hoof dressings without asking your farrier's or vet's advice, as some may not be suitable for your horse's feet.

Cosmetic hoof dressings are painted on just before competitions.

Shoeing a horse

Horses are shod to enable them to work in comfort. Sometimes special studs are screwed into the shoes to give extra grip for jumping and galloping.

Horseshoe nails have flat, square heads.

Well-shaped hoof in good condition that has been recently shod

WHEN TO SHOE
Horses and ponies should have their shoes removed and their hooves trimmed every six weeks. Worn shoes should be replaced.

WELL-SHOD HOOF
The shoe should be shaped to fit the hoof, not the other way around. Nailing the shoes on does not hurt the horse.

The farrier

A farrier, who makes horseshoes and shoes horses, needs a dry, well-lit area in which to work. Horses can be shod cold or hot. Both methods use nails to keep the shoe in place, however during hot shoeing the shoe is burnt on, which often gives a better fit.

The farrier will appreciate a quiet, well-mannered horse.

Curved knife, called drawing knife, for trimming hoof

Protective leather apron on which farrier can rest horse's leg

Frog is sensitive and must not be punctured.

The horse should be ready when the farrier arrives, and have clean legs and hooves.

Hind hooves are slightly smaller than front hooves.

CLIPPING

HORSES ARE CLIPPED if their winter coats are too thick for them to work or be ridden without sweating. A horse may need several clips during one season. The type of clip depends on the horse's lifestyle and workload; the more work it does, the less winter coat it should have. A clipped horse needs to wear blankets indoors and out so that it is warm when not working. Some horses are nervous when clipped, and must be handled by experts.

NATURAL COATS
All horses and ponies grow winter coats. Breeds such as British native ponies have thicker winter coats, as protection against wind and rain, than horses with a lot of Thoroughbred or Arab blood, which are kept in stables.

Types of clip
There are several different types of clip. Sometimes a lot of hair is removed from horses that work hard. Those that perform lighter work, or that spend most of their time outdoors, need some of their natural coat left on.

HUNTER CLIP
The hunter clip is used on horses that work hard and fast. All of the coat is clipped except that on the legs and sometimes under the saddle.

Thick leg hair protects the horse against mud and thorns.

BLANKET CLIP
Leaving a blanket-shaped area over the back of the horse unclipped helps keep the horse's back warm. Hair is also left on the legs, but is clipped off the neck. This type of clip allows a hard-working horse to keep cool.

Clipping a horse

Always clip a horse in a dry, light area, and never outdoors when it is wet or windy. Be careful when using electric clippers – they can be dangerous. Only experts should clip inexperienced or nervous horses.

Trim the hair from the edges of the horse's ears only, not inside.

Keep the folded blanket on the pony so it does not get cold.

Clip in smooth sweeps against the direction of the hair growth.

Someone holds the horse and gives it confidence while another person clips.

Care of a clipped horse

A clipped horse must be kept warm and dry with blankets. If kept indoors, a horse must have a well ventilated, but not drafty, area. Blankets with neck covers and tail flaps give extra protection. A fully-clipped horse may need to wear an exercise sheet when out riding.

Before putting the blanket on remove loose hair.

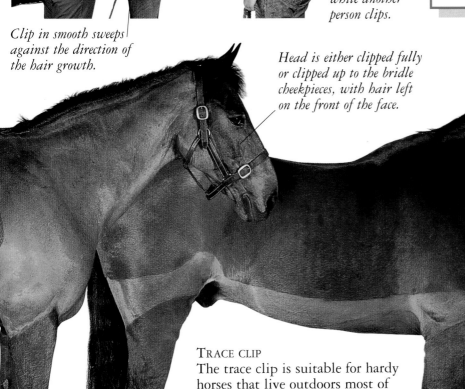

Head is either clipped fully or clipped up to the bridle cheekpieces, with hair left on the front of the face.

Coat is clipped off the underside of the neck, where horses often sweat.

TRACE CLIP
The trace clip is suitable for hardy horses that live outdoors most of the time. It reduces sweating but leaves some protection. The trace clip gets its name because it was designed for harness horses and follows the lines of the harness traces.

A trace-clipped horse may need to wear a blanket when resting.

BLANKETS AND BLANKETING

A BLANKET KEEPS A HORSE warm and dry in cold weather. In summer, light blankets, or sheets, protect horses from insects. Blankets also help to dry off a sweating horse, or if a horse is very wet, they can help it warm up and dry off more quickly. The main types of blanket are outdoor or New Zealand rugs, stable blankets, summer sheets, coolers, and sweat sheets.

Measuring up

A blanket must be the correct size to stay in place. Measure the horse from the center of its chest in a straight line across its body. This will give you the length your horse needs.

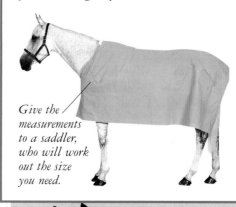

Give the measurements to a saddler, who will work out the size you need.

Putting on a blanket

A horse's coat must lie flat under its blanket so it is comfortable. The fastenings must be tight enough to keep the blanket in place, but not so tight they restrict or cut into the horse.

Modern blankets are machine washable. Keep them clean to prevent skin problems.

A high-cut blanket on the neck will be less likely to slip backward than one which is cut low on the neck.

1 Place the blanket Fold the blanket in half from the back to the front and place it over the withers. Slide the blanket back so the horse's coat lies flat underneath, and fold down the back half.

The blanket should not press on the horse's chest.

Types of blanket

There are many different types of blankets. A stable blanket keeps the horse warm and clean. It is easy to wash and can be worn daily. Summer sheets are made of light cotton to keep dust and flies off a stabled, groomed horse. Sweat sheets and coolers allow the horse's sweat to evaporate.

Stable blankets do not need to be waterproof. You may need to use more than one blanket on your horse as the weather gets very cold.

Outdoor or New Zealand rugs must be waterproof. They are available in canvas and many modern lightweight materials.

Summer sheets are usually made from cotton.

Traditional sweat sheets are used with a blanket or summer sheet laid over the top, to trap a layer of air.

Blanket should cover the withers at the front.

Cross surcingles help prevent excess pressure on horse's spine.

Some surcingles are elasticated.

2 Fasten the front straps
Fasten the blanket leaving a hand's width between the blanket and the horse's body.

3 Fasten the cross surcingles
The cross surcingles fasten around the horse's girth. Adjust the straps leaving a hand's width between them and the horse.

HEALTH AND FIRST AID

REGULAR DEWORMING, teeth rasping, and vaccinations against influenza and tetanus are vital to keep a horse healthy. Your vet can advise you about these. Learn to recognize when a horse might be ill, and how to take its temperature, and check its pulse and respiration (breathing) rate. If in doubt or worried, always call a vet.

STERILE PAD

SCISSORS

COLD TREATMENT PACK

ANTISEPTIC LIQUID

FIRST AID KIT
Keep a first-aid kit at the stable and take it with you when you go to shows. Your vet will advise you what to include in the kit.

Eyes should be fully open and bright, with no discharge.

Checking your horse
Check your horse every day for signs of injury or illness. As you get to know your horse you will be able to tell if it is not well. A healthy horse is alert and appears happy.

A sore back can be a sign of a badly fitting saddle.

Tail should be relaxed, not clamped down.

Look out for cuts and grazes that may need attention.

Check for any signs of heat or swelling in legs.

If one hoof is warmer than its pair, it may indicate a problem.

TROTTING UP
Lameness usually shows in a trot but not a walk. Trot up your horse on hard, flat ground. A lame horse's head rises as the lame leg hits the ground and sinks as the sound one comes down.

Preventing illness

It is better to prevent disease than to have to treat it once it occurs. All horses should be dewormed and vaccinated regularly. They should also have their teeth checked and rasped at least once a year. Daily checks and correct management and feeding help prevent illness.

Paste wormers are put on the back of the horse's tongue using a syringe.

CHECKING PULSE
A normal pulse in an adult horse ranges from 35 to 45 beats per minute. The pulse will be faster in hot weather or when the horse has worked hard.

One of the easiest places to take the pulse is where the facial artery crosses the horse's jaw bone.

DEWORMING
Horses should be dewormed every few weeks. There are many different types of worms; ask your vet's advice on which types of wormers to use and when to give them.

WHEN TO CALL THE VET

Always call the vet if you are worried about something, however small. Suspected colic or laminitis, or wounds spurting blood, are always emergencies. A vet should always be called if lameness is severe or prolonged, or if a wound may need stitching.

COMMON AILMENTS

COLIC	SIGNS OF COLIC	GENERALLY SICK
Colic is another word for abdominal pain or stomach ache. Horses cannot be sick, so colic is always serious. Call your vet as soon as you suspect that something is wrong. Some cases may need surgery.	*Sweating, rolling, and kicking at the belly are all signs of colic.*	Always call your vet if you think your horse might need treatment. Describe the symptoms or injury carefully. With suspected illness, it may be useful to take the horse's temperature.
BAD CUT Any cut that is longer than 1 in (2.5 cm) or gapes open may need stitching. Puncture wounds and those near joints may also need veterinary attention. Be safe, not sorry!	**LAMINITIS** Laminitis is a painful hoof condition that is especially common in ponies. It is often linked to eating rich grass and usually affects the front hooves, so the pony tries to put more weight on its back ones. Your vet may recommend special shoes for your pony to wear.	**ARTERIAL BLEEDING** If bright red blood spurts from a wound, your horse has probably severed an artery. Press a clean cloth firmly over the wound to limit the bleeding until the vet arrives.
PROLONGED LAMENESS Always rest a lame horse. If very mild lameness lasts for more than two days, or if you are unsure, call your vet. Conditions such as tendon injuries or pulled muscles can get worse and need immediate treatment, so again, call your vet.	**SITES OF LAMENESS** *Most causes of lameness occur in the hoof, such as bruises and puncture wounds.*	**SEVERE LAMENESS** A horse that is very lame or unable to put its injured hoof on the ground is an emergency case. With suspected fractures, try to keep the horse still until the vet arrives. This prevents the injury from getting worse.

CARE OF TACK

TACK MUST BE KEPT CLEAN and in good repair. Wash the bit and clean off dried mud every time you ride. If you don't take care of your tack it will become hard and cracked and uncomfortable for the horse to wear. At least once a week, more often if possible, dismantle the tack and clean thoroughly.

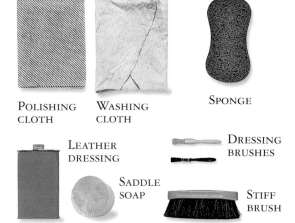

POLISHING CLOTH WASHING CLOTH SPONGE

LEATHER DRESSING DRESSING BRUSHES

SADDLE SOAP STIFF BRUSH

Tack

Every horse should have its own tack. Make sure the tack fits properly; get expert advice if you are not sure. Saddles and bridles are made from either leather or synthetic materials. Keep tack in a dry, warm place, away from damp. Dry rain soaked leather tack away from direct heat otherwise it may turn brittle.

To hang a bridle use a special bridle rack or make your own from a round tin.

Wash bits in clean water.

Don't use metal polish on mouthpiece.

Only use saddle soap on leather reins.

Too much soap on the saddle seat may stain clothes.

Wash synthetic girths as often as is necessary.

TACK CLEANING KIT
For general tack cleaning you need warm water, cloths and sponges, and a stiff brush to remove dirt. Use saddle soap to keep the tack supple, and apply leather dressing about once a month, especially if the tack is new.

Synthetic tack
Some synthetic tack, especially bridles and girths, comes in bright, cheerful colors. Synthetic tack should be wiped with a damp cloth or washed according to the manufacturer's instructions.

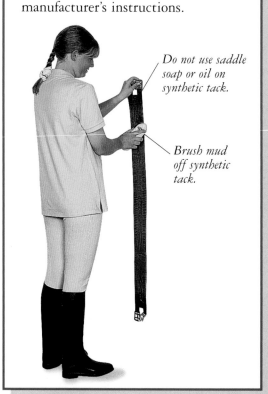

Do not use saddle soap or oil on synthetic tack.

Brush mud off synthetic tack.

SADDLE CARE
Keep your saddle on a special rack or stand to help prevent it from getting damaged. As with all tack, the saddle should always be kept in a dry room.

Scrub dirt from stirrup treads, then wash and dry stirrup irons.

Remove girth for cleaning.

In the tack room

Your tack room should be dry, warm, and secure. It is a good idea to install security equipment, such as alarms and a good lock. It is in the tack room that you usually clean the tack. To do this remove grease and dirt with a damp cloth, then apply saddle soap with a slightly damp sponge. Wash and rinse bits and stirrup irons, then polish with a dry cloth. Brush or wash girths and saddle pads.

The pommel and cantle, at the front and back of a saddle, are easily damaged.

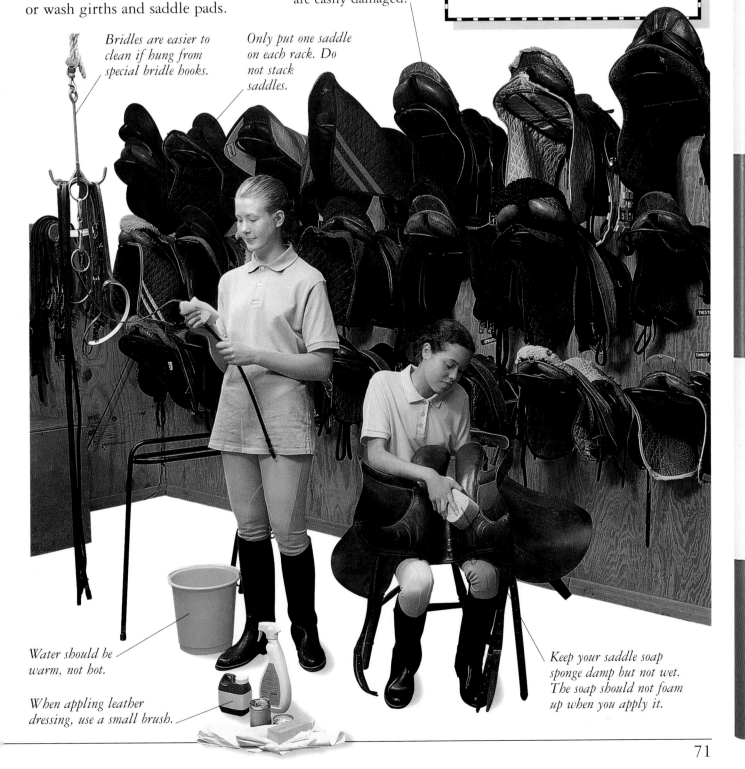

Bridles are easier to clean if hung from special bridle hooks.

Only put one saddle on each rack. Do not stack saddles.

Water should be warm, not hot.

When appling leather dressing, use a small brush.

Keep your saddle soap sponge damp but not wet. The soap should not foam up when you apply it.

TRANSPORTING A HORSE

WHEN TRANSPORTING a horse in a trailer you must aways protect it with traveling equipment, even for short journeys. The trailer should be in good condition and be large enough for a horse to travel comfortably. Horses should be tied up, but foals travel loose with their mothers. The driver should try to drive as smoothly as possible.

Protecting the horse

A horse should always wear travel boots or leg wraps over padding. A tail bandage or tailguard and a blanket suitable for the weather conditions are also essential.

Blanket protects horse from drafts in hot weather.

Loading up

When loading the horse into the trailer, open up the vehicle as much as possible so the horse can see where it is being asked to go. Make sure the ramp is secure, then lead the horse straight up it. Look ahead into the trailer, not back at the horse. Tie the horse up so it cannot turn around.

The vehicle interior should be light and inviting as horses do not like walking into dark places.

Provide a small haynet to prevent horse becoming bored during the journey.

WARNING!
Only load into an unhitched trailer if the rear prop stands are lowered.

Ramp must be stable, not tipped up at one side.

Check that tire pressures are correct before every journey.

HORSE TRAVEL

- Always put traveling equipment on a horse, even for a short journey

- Vehicle should be light, airy, and in good condition

- Allow plenty of time for loading, unloading, and traveling so the horse is calm when it arrives

- Give the horse a haynet in the vehicle to encourage it to relax on the journey

- Driver should make all changes in speed and direction as smooth as possible

Unloading

The vehicle should be parked so that the horse has plenty of room to turn when it walks off the ramp. Make sure the ramp is stable, and lead the horse straight out so it does not bang against the side of the trailer.

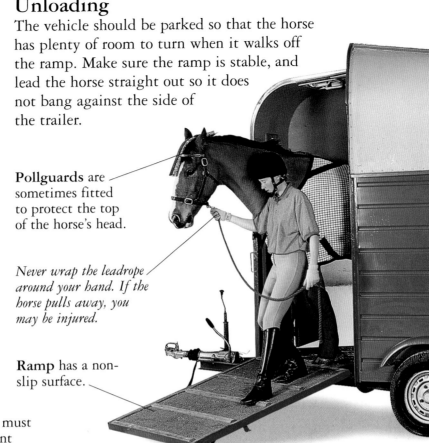

Pollguards are sometimes fitted to protect the top of the horse's head.

Never wrap the leadrope around your hand. If the horse pulls away, you may be injured.

Ramp has a non-slip surface.

Roof height must allow sufficient headroom for the horse.

Wear a hard hat when loading unknown or unpredictable horses.

Always outfit a traveling horse with a suitable blanket or sheet.

Tail bandage or tailguard protects tail hair from rubbing.

Leg wraps or bandages prevent leg injuries.

73

SAFETY

YOUR HORSE'S SAFETY depends on you, so check the pasture and stable area every day to make sure they are clean and safe, thus helping to prevent illness or injury. It is also important to care for your own safety by handling horses correctly and never taking risks – even quiet horses may be unpredictable if they are sick or frightened. First-aid kits for both horses and people should always be available.

First aid for riders

Every stable should have first-aid kits for riders. Your doctor can advise you on what to include in a first-aid kit. A telephone should also be available, with emergency numbers displayed.

First-aid kit includes bandages, ointments, and scissors.

Safety at the stable

The buildings and stalls must be kept in good repair, and tools and equipment should be stored safely when not in use. Dogs and young children should be supervised and not allowed to run around.

Stay calm and concentrate on what you are doing. Never take risks.

Ears laid back show that the horse is unhappy.

Horses can kick forward and backward.

A horse may kick out, so always stand to one side of it.

HORSE BEHAVIOR

A frightened horse will try to run away and one that is in pain may kick or be difficult to handle. When near the horse, always stand in a safe position. If you have to do something the horse may object to, tie up the horse. If necessary, ask for help.

KEEPING YOUR HORSE SAFE

Daily checking of the pasture and fencing, and careful stable management will help you create a safe environment for your horse. By performing these checks you will minimize the risks to your horse of both illness and injury, for example from broken fencing. It is also important to take precautions against theft and fire.

IN THE STABLE

STABLE MANAGEMENT
Keep the stable clean and dust-free. Provide the horse with a deep bed, so that it doesn't injure itself on the stable floor. Disinfect the floor and walls at least twice a year. Wash buckets every day.

SECURITY
Protect your horse from theft by using a security marking system such as freeze marking. Mark tack and equipment with your name or address. Stable your horse where someone lives on site.

FIRE PRECAUTIONS
Keep a fire extinguisher and hose in clear view so that everyone can see where they are. Make sure electricity supplies are safe and kept away from water sources.

KEEPING STABLE IN GOOD REPAIR
Stables should be kept in good repair so that there are no visible nails, broken wood, or other sharp objects that could injure a horse. Doors should have latches at top and bottom, so that they can be shut tight when the horse is in the stable.

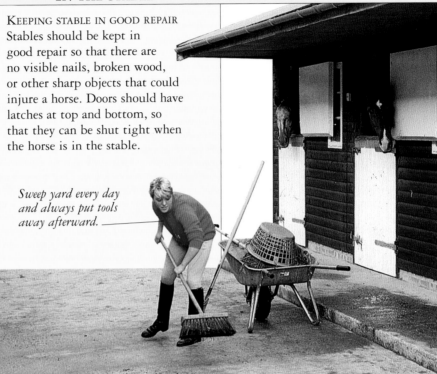

Sweep yard every day and always put tools away afterward.

AT PASTURE

Always provide clean water.

CHECKING WATER SUPPLY
Use a container that horses cannot knock over to provide a constant supply of clean water. These should not have any sharp edges or projections that could injure a horse. Keep container free from debris, such as fallen leaves, and if necessary, break any ice.

FILLING IN HOLES
Use spare soil to fill in holes in the pasture made by rabbits, moles, or other animals. If a horse puts its foot down a hole it could break its leg. If your pasture has a lot of holes, get expert advice on pest control.

KEEPING THE PASTURE CLEAN
Remove manure as often as possible, preferably every day. This helps to reduce the amount of worm eggs that live in horse manure, thus lessening health risks to the horse. Get advice on harrowing large pastures.

REMOVING POISONOUS PLANTS
Learn to identify poisonous plants such as ragwort, yew, and deadly nightshade. Remove and burn them. Acorns are poisonous, so fence off oak trees and their surroundings.

CHECKING FENCING
Check fencing daily for weak or broken parts. Electric fencing must be correctly installed; check that nothing is touching the electrified parts, thus causing a short circuit. If you are unsure, ask an expert how to use electric fencing.

HORSE CARE

ROUTINE CARE, such as grooming, is the responsibility of those looking after a horse or pony – usually you. Other tasks, such as vaccinating, must be done by qualified professionals. Never forget preventative measures such as deworming, or your horse's health will suffer.

JOB	DESCRIPTION
SIGNS OF ILL HEALTH	Always be alert for signs that a horse may be sick or injured. Danger signs include heat or swelling in the legs, restlessness and sweating, eye or nasal discharge, labored breathing, and listlessness.
DEWORMING	Deworming is giving a medical paste from syringes directly into a horse's mouth, or putting granules into the feed. The vet will advise you on which products to use.
VACCINATE	All horses should be vaccinated against tetanus and equine influenza. Brood mares may need extra vaccinations, so check with the vet.
SHOEING	All horses should have their hooves trimmed regularly to prevent them growing too long. Most horses need to wear shoes if they are ridden regularly.
RASP TEETH	Sharp teeth and hooks (curved projections on a tooth) are filed down using special dental equipment.
CHECK PASTURE	Check the pasture for broken or weak fencing and repair when needed. Remove and burn poisonous plants and any trash. Fill in holes made by small animals. Remove manure.
GROOMING	Stabled horses need to be groomed thoroughly. Pastured horses need coat oils for protection, so just brush off dried mud and groom mane and tail.
CLIPPING	This is the removal of all, or parts, of a horse's winter coat, using special electric or battery-operated equine clippers.
TACK FIT	Check that the bit, bridle, and saddle are the correct size and tack is not damaged or faulty.

Trotting up horse to observe its movement.

Feeding a pony

Blankets need to be put on horses that are clipped or have thin winter coats. A sick horse will need rugs to keep it warm. Take off and replace blankets at least once a day.

PUTTING ON A BLANKET

CLEANING OUT TOOLS

Cleaning out every day keeps a horse's stall free from harmful gases given off by wet, dirty bedding. Store tools safely after use.

FREQUENCY	WHO DOES IT	WHY
Each time you see the pony, especially first thing in the morning.	You or anyone else responsible for the horse's care.	The sooner potential problems are spotted, the more likely it is that the horse will make a quick recovery. In colic cases, speedy action can save a horse's life.
Every six to eight weeks on veterinary advice.	You – ask someone to show you how to administer paste.	All horses have some worms in their intestines. Deworming reduces the amount of worms in the body to a safe level.
A primary course is followed by annual boosters.	Vet	To protect horses against conditions that can, at times, be fatal.
Every four to six weeks.	A farrier. Only a registered farrier can shoe horses.	Domestic horses' hooves do not wear down fast enough, unlike those of wild horses, which are constantly on the move.
Once or twice a year, depending on needs of individual horse.	Vet or trained equine dentist.	Rasping teeth helps keep a horse comfortable when it is wearing a bit. It also improves a horse's ability to chew and digest food.
Every day	You or anyone else responsible for the horse's care.	Check the pasture to keep horse from escaping and to prevent injury or illness. Removing manure helps reduce amount of worms.
Every day	You or anyone else responsible for the horse's care.	Helps keep coat and skin healthy and helps you spot wounds, heat, or swelling.
Up to three times a year once horse's winter coat is fully grown.	Must be done by an experienced adult.	Enables horse to work without sweating too much.
Check for safety every time you ride. Check saddle fit every month.	Always get expert advice, especially for saddles and bits.	Badly fitting tack can cause discomfort, injury, and poor performance.

Cleaning the nose

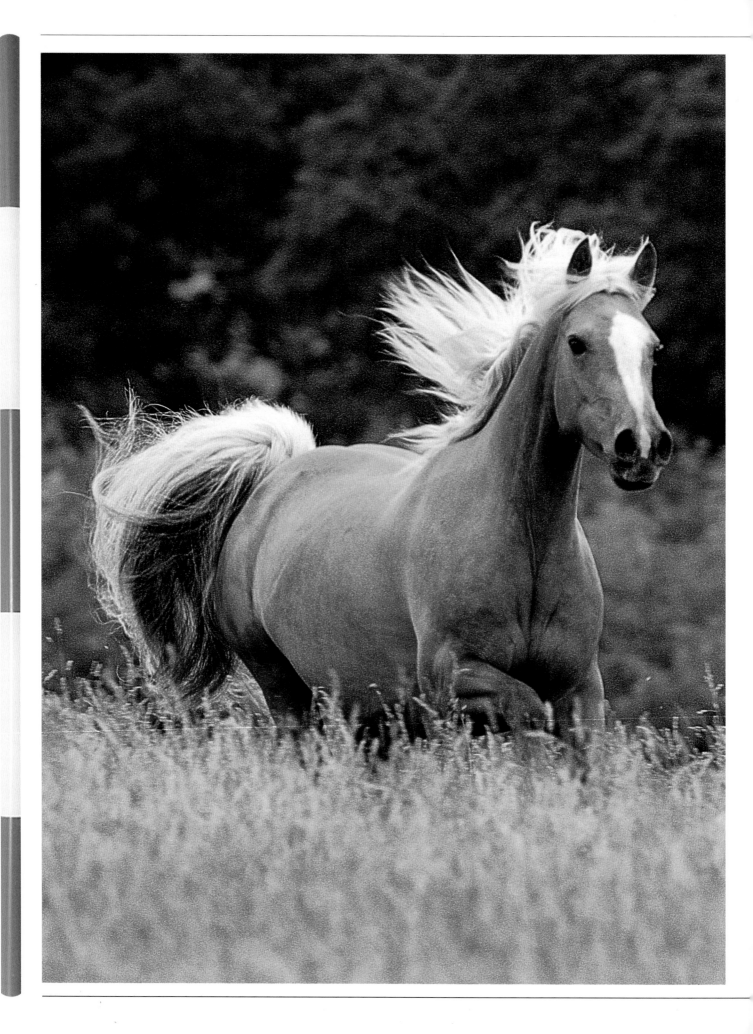

HORSE & PONY BREEDS

ORIGINS

THERE ARE MORE than 75 breeds of horses and ponies. All can be traced back to the same ancestors that appeared on Earth 60 million years ago. By the time the horse was domesticated about 6,000 years ago, there were four types of horses. From these types developed certain breeds such as the Arabian, which have had a great impact on the development of modern horses.

THE FIRST HORSE
Eohippus, or the Dawn horse, was about 14 in (36 cm) high. It had four toes on each front foot, and three on the hind foot. *Eohippus* fed on leaves, since there was no grass.

The greatest influences

The three main influences on modern riding horses and ponies are the Arabian, the Barb, and the Thoroughbred. The Arabian and the Barb are the oldest of these, though scientists are not sure which came first. The Thoroughbred is the most recent influence, and has also had the strongest effect.

The Barb is deep and strong through the body, and has either a straight or slightly convex head.

The third toe became larger until the side toes eventually disappeared.

Longer leg, with single hoof

Four toes on front foot of early horse

The Barb
The Barb played a major part in the development of many European breeds, such as the Andalusian. Like the Arabian, it is a desert horse, but it is not as beautiful or graceful. It lacks the Arabian's very concave face and high-set tail.

EVOLUTION OF THE FOOT
The horse's foot developed as the landscape changed from swamp to plains. Its longer limbs and single hoof gave it speed on the open grasslands.

Dense coat protects against cold and wet.

EXMOOR

Heavy build helps to cope with cold and frost.

Coarser limbs and feathers

HIGHLAND

Pony type 1

Found in northwestern Europe, this type was about 12.2 hh. It had a straight profile and small ears. This hardy pony was highly resistant to wet and able to thrive in harsh conditions. The Exmoor pony is its nearest modern equivalent.

Pony type 2

Standing at about 14.2 hh, this type was heavily built and coarse in appearance. Its head was large in relation to its body. This pony settled in northern Eurasia, where it was able to survive the cold. The Highland pony is its nearest equivalent.

Thin neck is set very high and supports head with fine ears.

This type had a long, narrow body and was lean and thin-skinned.

AKHAL-TEKE

Refined build and slim body

Concave head, characteristics of both the Arabian and Caspian pony

CASPIAN

Horse type 3

A horse rather than a pony, this horse type stood at about 15 hh. It had a long body, long neck, and long ears, and was shallow through the girth. Living in central Asia, it was resistant to heat and drought. The Akhal-Teke is the modern breed that resembles it most closely.

Horse type 4

This type was a pony in terms of height, but a miniature horse in terms of conformation. It had a concave face and a high-set tail. A concave face is a characteristic of both the Arabian and Caspian pony; some scientists believe that horse type 4 was the blueprint for these breeds.

THE MODERN HORSE

MODERN HORSES and ponies are bred for specific functions. These range from pleasure riding, driving, and working on the land, to competing in specialized sports such as dressage, racing, and show jumping. Horses can be classified by breed, type, color, and markings. A horse bred for one type of activity may not be suitable for another; some, however, are adaptable and have many uses.

Warmbloods

Warmbloods are the ultimate modern sport horses. They combine Thoroughbred, or hot blood, with cold blood, or heavier horse, influences. Warmbloods are the result of careful breeding programs.

Only proven performance horses are used to breed warmbloods.

Classification of the horse

The two main types of horse are heavy and light. Ponies form a third group. Heavy horses include the largest, most powerful breeds, and often reach more than 17 hh. Light horse breeds and types, such as riding horses, are more than 14.2 hh, while ponies are 14.2 hh or less.

CLYDESDALE

Braided mane is traditional.

HEAVY HORSES

Heavy breeds are the giants of the horse world. They have been bred to work on the land and have broad, strong backs and powerful legs. The angle of the shoulder is often straighter than in light horse breeds, which gives the heavier horses great pulling power.

Powerful hindquarters for speed

Well-proportioned hind legs

Feathers protect skin on powerful forelegs when plodding through mud.

COLORS AND MARKINGS

Colors and markings are key identification points for horses and ponies. Colors can be solid or broken, and some horses, such as Palominos, are bred specifically for their color. Face and leg markings are white patches on a solid color, such as bay or chestnut.

COLORS

COAT COLORINGS
Color is determined by the horse's genetic makeup. Some colors are always dominant. For example, if one parent is gray and the other is either bay, black, or chestnut, the foal will always be gray. There are also classifications within the colors, so a Paint may be called a tobiano or an overo depending on the distribution of solid color compared to white.

DUN

PALOMINO

PAINT

SPOTTED

CHESTNUT

PAINT

BAY

DAPPLE GRAY

MARKINGS

FACE AND LEG MARKINGS
The most common face markings are stars, stripes, snips, or combinations of these. A white or bald face covers the forehead and front of the face. Leg markings include socks, which extend up to the knees, while stockings run further up the leg.

STRIPE

STAR

STOCKING

SOCK

ERMINE

THOROUGHBRED

Fine coat and slender build help horse to stay cool.

Bushy mane protects pony against cold and wet weather.

WELSH PONY

Long, sloping shoulder indicates good movement and a comfortable ride.

Body is compact with depth through the girth.

LIGHT HORSE
The light horse riding breeds and types always have some Thoroughbred blood. Their body shape and movement makes them comfortable to ride.

PONY
Different pony breeds have height restrictions and definite characteristics depending on the type of work for which they were traditionally used. Many are tough and hardy.

Short forearms help bear weight.

PHYSICAL FEATURES

THE HORSE HAS acute senses, which, together with its physical characteristics and shape, enable it to spot potential dangers and flee. Correct conformation, or shape, is not just important because it makes the horse beautiful; if the horse's body and legs have the right proportions and angles, it will be more likely to stay sound and be athletic. No horse is perfect, but its strengths should outweigh its weaknesses.

Conformation

A well-made horse has good hooves and legs to support its body easily. Its back, quarters, and hind legs should be strong, and its body deep for efficient heart and lung function. A sloping shoulder angle helps the riding horse move gracefully.

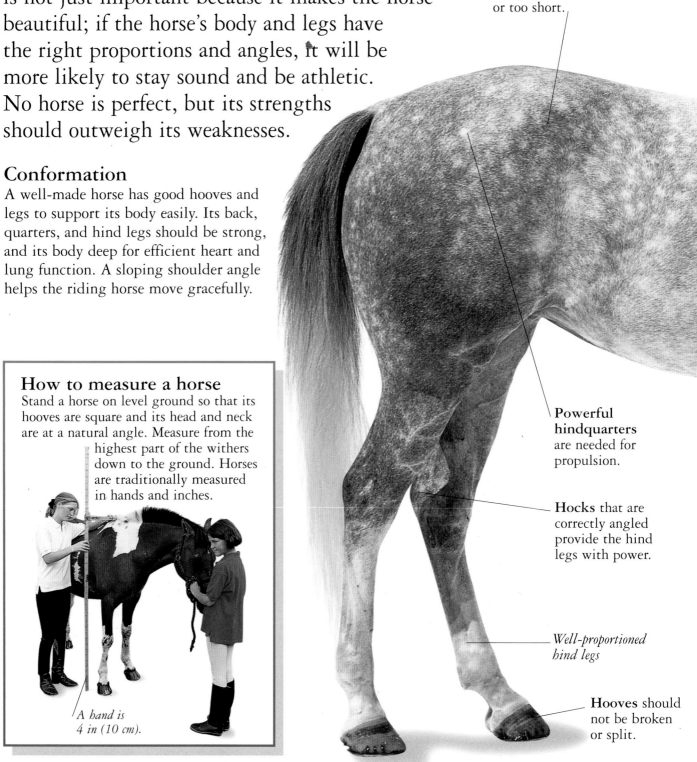

Strong loins and back give strength. The back must not be too long or too short.

Powerful hindquarters are needed for propulsion.

Hocks that are correctly angled provide the hind legs with power.

Well-proportioned hind legs

Hooves should not be broken or split.

How to measure a horse
Stand a horse on level ground so that its hooves are square and its head and neck are at a natural angle. Measure from the highest part of the withers down to the ground. Horses are traditionally measured in hands and inches.

A hand is 4 in (10 cm).

Neck is at the correct angle from the withers, so the horse finds it easier to balance.

Head is in proportion the with rest of the body and the ears are alert.

Sloping shoulder for good movement and ride.

POOR CONFORMATION
When a horse's body is not suitable for the work it is expected to do, it is said to have poor conformation. Common faults are bad hooves and weak legs. A horse with a kind, willing temperament may compensate for small imperfections.

Eyes should be large and bright to indicate calm temperament and intelligence.

Nostrils are not flared while horse is at rest.

Body and head are streamlined.

Skin is supple and elastic. Coat is smooth and shiny.

Deep body gives heart and lungs plenty of room.

Well-formed joints

Sloping pastern

Cranium   *Orbit*   *Nasal bone*

Lumbar vertebrae

Thoracic vertebrae

Cervical vertebrae

Sacrum

Atlas

Femur

Scapular spine

Stifle joint

Humerus

Fibula

Rib cage

Hock bones

Tibia

Radius

Fetlock joint

Cannon bone

Coffin joint

BODY SUPPORT
The horse's skeleton is made up of bones and cartilage. There are two parts to the skeleton. The axial skeleton, which consists of the skull, backbone, sternum, and ribs, protects the brain, spinal cord, and internal organs. The appendicular skeleton, which supports the body, comprises the shoulders, forelegs, pelvic girdle, and hind legs.

HORSE AND PONY TYPES

HORSES CAN BE classified by type as well as breed. Sometimes a horse's breeding is unspecific, but its conformation, build, and movement make it a particular type. Types have a set of physical characteristics that help them perform specific functions, such as hunting, hacking, or farming. However, some breeds have a powerful influence on types. For example, Thoroughbred blood gives quality and extra agility to riding and sport horses, while most cobs have some draft horse ancestry.

Different types
Some horses, such as cobs, hunters, and hacks, fulfill a particular purpose, but do not belong to a specific breed. When horses of the same type breed, their offspring will often, but not always, have the same characteristics.

Domestic horses
For many centuries, all horses were wild. They were not domesticated until about 6,000 years ago. Today, although the Camargue horses of southern France live in the wild, they are kept in herds and used to work the area's black cattle. The only truly wild horse is Przewalski's horse.

A calm temperament is essential for riding horses.

RIDING HORSE
The ideal riding horse is a perfectly proportioned light horse. It usually has at least 50 percent Thoroughbred.

Hind legs are fine, but strong

Feathers are clipped off riding cobs.

Hooves are good-sized for working on rough ground.

COB
The cob is a deep-bodied horse with short legs. It has a great weight-carrying ability and was originally used by farmers. Show cobs must be more than 14.2 hh, but must not exceed 15.1 hh.

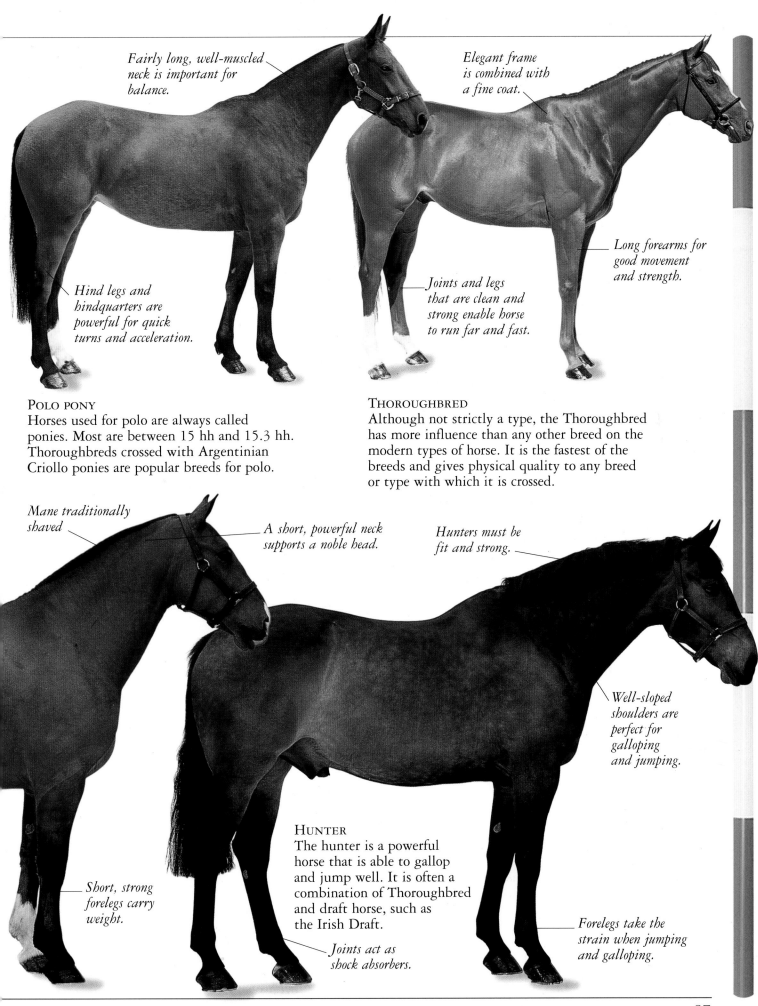

Fairly long, well-muscled neck is important for balance.

Elegant frame is combined with a fine coat.

Long forearms for good movement and strength.

Hind legs and hindquarters are powerful for quick turns and acceleration.

Joints and legs that are clean and strong enable horse to run far and fast.

POLO PONY
Horses used for polo are always called ponies. Most are between 15 hh and 15.3 hh. Thoroughbreds crossed with Argentinian Criollo ponies are popular breeds for polo.

THOROUGHBRED
Although not strictly a type, the Thoroughbred has more influence than any other breed on the modern types of horse. It is the fastest of the breeds and gives physical quality to any breed or type with which it is crossed.

Mane traditionally shaved

A short, powerful neck supports a noble head.

Hunters must be fit and strong.

Well-sloped shoulders are perfect for galloping and jumping.

Short, strong forelegs carry weight.

HUNTER
The hunter is a powerful horse that is able to gallop and jump well. It is often a combination of Thoroughbred and draft horse, such as the Irish Draft.

Joints act as shock absorbers.

Forelegs take the strain when jumping and galloping.

THE ARABIAN

THE ARABIAN is one of the oldest breeds and is often described as the most beautiful horse in the world. It is recognized by its short, refined head and high tail carriage. When crossed with other breeds, these characteristics are often passed on, though to a lesser extent. Tough, hardy, and fast, the Arabian excels in racing and endurance sports. It is sensitive and intelligent.

Legends and history
The Arabian can be traced back 3,000 years, although legend says it was created by Allah from handfuls of the north and south winds. Bedouin tribesmen allowed their favorite Arabian mares to live in their tents. Artists have always been captivated by the Arabian's beauty.

Arabian versatility
Arabians are hardy and athletic horses with naturally good balance. They are not fashionable for dressage because of their high head and tail carriage, but can perform difficult movements as well as any other breed. Their long stride, great speed, and tough hooves make them naturally good at endurance sports.

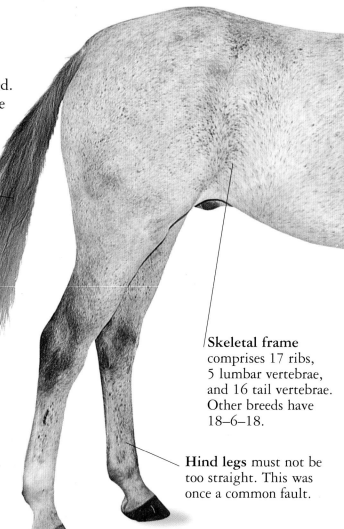

High-set tail

Skeletal frame comprises 17 ribs, 5 lumbar vertebrae, and 16 tail vertebrae. Other breeds have 18–6–18.

Hind legs must not be too straight. This was once a common fault.

THE ARABIAN

- Seventeen ribs compared to 18 in other breeds, so it is short-backed

- Bone is denser and stronger than in other breeds

- Mane and tail hair is fine and very silky

- Colors are gray, bay, chestnut, and black

- Muzzle is small with large, flared nostrils

- Legs are long and slender

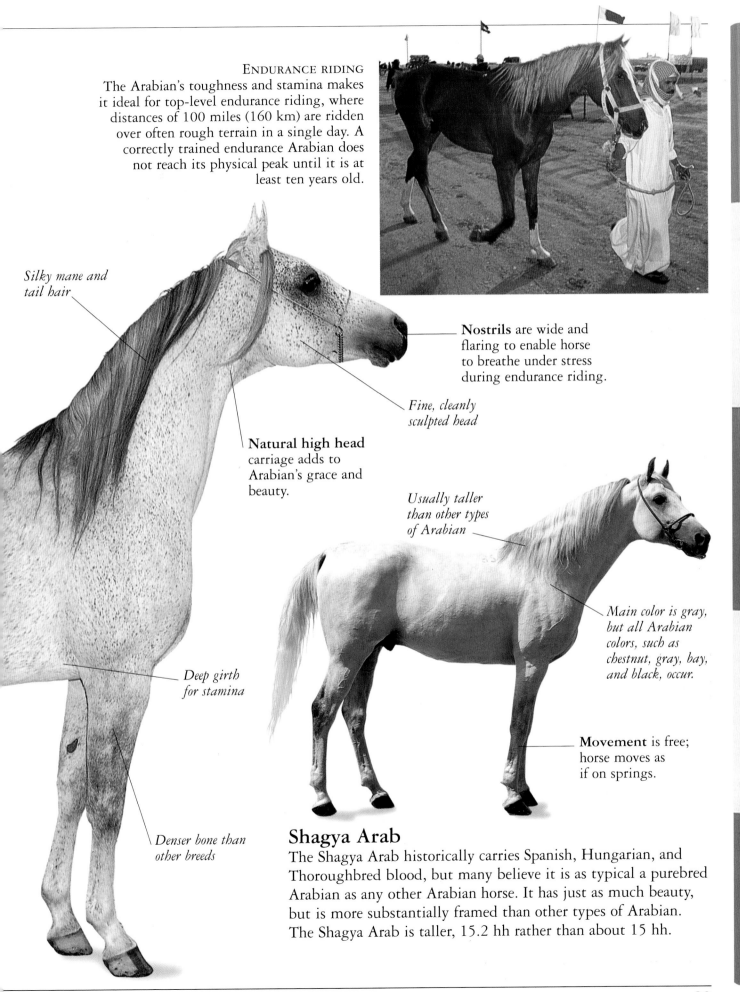

The Arabian's toughness and stamina makes it ideal for top-level endurance riding, where distances of 100 miles (160 km) are ridden over often rough terrain in a single day. A correctly trained endurance Arabian does not reach its physical peak until it is at least ten years old.

Silky mane and tail hair

Nostrils are wide and flaring to enable horse to breathe under stress during endurance riding.

Fine, cleanly sculpted head

Natural high head carriage adds to Arabian's grace and beauty.

Usually taller than other types of Arabian

Main color is gray, but all Arabian colors, such as chestnut, gray, bay, and black, occur.

Deep girth for stamina

Movement is free; horse moves as if on springs.

Denser bone than other breeds

Shagya Arab

The Shagya Arab historically carries Spanish, Hungarian, and Thoroughbred blood, but many believe it is as typical a purebred Arabian as any other Arabian horse. It has just as much beauty, but is more substantially framed than other types of Arabian. The Shagya Arab is taller, 15.2 hh rather than about 15 hh.

SPANISH HORSES

THE ANDALUSIAN, which has been known for centuries as the Spanish horse, is the third greatest influence on modern horse and pony breeds. Its beauty and power, combined with a bold but willing temperament, have made it the mount of bullfighters, classical dressage riders, and enthusiasts throughout the world. The Lusitano and the Lipizzan also have strong Spanish influences.

HARNESS CHAMPIONS
The Andalusian, Lusitano, and Lipizzan are all spectacular carriage horses and are also highly prized as riding horses. Their good movement is combined with a trainable temperament.

The Andalusian

The Andalusian is a powerful horse with a substantial frame that makes it look bigger than its average 15.2 hh. Its movement is controlled and high stepping. Strong hindquarters give it a natural ability for advanced dressage movements.

Hindquarters are particularly strong.

Coat color is usually gray or bay.

Powerful hock joints add strength.

Knee joints should be large and flat for soundness and toughness.

Tail is long, luxurious, and often wavy.

SPANISH HORSES

- Once unfashionable, these breeds are now finding favor with some dressage riders

- All three breeds are usually gray

- Kind temperament means that stallions are favored for riding

- Mares are traditionally used only for breeding

- The Alter Real is a breed that also descends from Andalusian stock

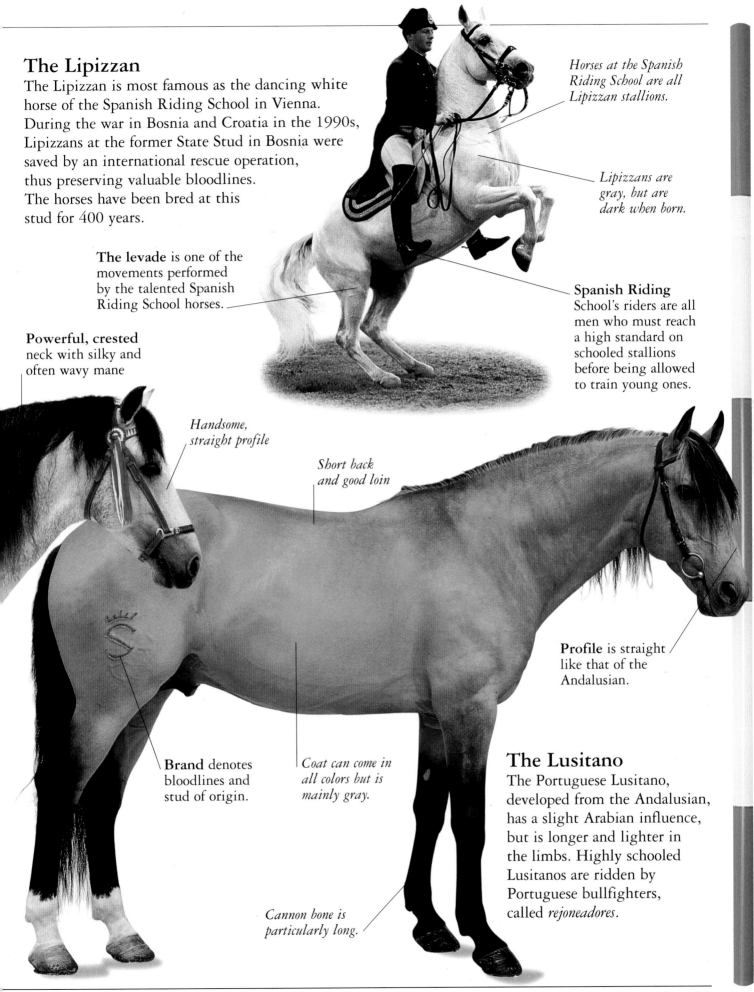

The Lipizzan

The Lipizzan is most famous as the dancing white horse of the Spanish Riding School in Vienna. During the war in Bosnia and Croatia in the 1990s, Lipizzans at the former State Stud in Bosnia were saved by an international rescue operation, thus preserving valuable bloodlines. The horses have been bred at this stud for 400 years.

Horses at the Spanish Riding School are all Lipizzan stallions.

Lipizzans are gray, but are dark when born.

The levade is one of the movements performed by the talented Spanish Riding School horses.

Spanish Riding School's riders are all men who must reach a high standard on schooled stallions before being allowed to train young ones.

Powerful, crested neck with silky and often wavy mane

Handsome, straight profile

Short back and good loin

Profile is straight like that of the Andalusian.

Brand denotes bloodlines and stud of origin.

Coat can come in all colors but is mainly gray.

The Lusitano

The Portuguese Lusitano, developed from the Andalusian, has a slight Arabian influence, but is longer and lighter in the limbs. Highly schooled Lusitanos are ridden by Portuguese bullfighters, called *rejoneadores*.

Cannon bone is particularly long.

THOROUGHBRED

THE THOROUGHBRED EVOLVED during the 17th and 18th centuries. It is the fastest and most valuable breed in the world, and is often crossed with other breeds to improve their quality. Thoroughbreds are generally bred for racing, but are also successful in horse trials and other sports.

Anglo-arab

The Anglo-arab is a cross between the two most influential breeds in the world, the Thoroughbred and the Arabian. It looks like the Thoroughbred in appearance, but ideally it should combine the speed of the Thoroughbred with the toughness of the Arabian, and share the beauty of both.

Thoroughbred

The Thoroughbred has had a strong influence on all breeds of modern competition horse. The best have great courage, mental stamina, and speed. They can be high-strung and usually have sharp reactions.

Fine, silky hair in mane, tail, and coat

ANGLO-ARAB

THOROUGHBRED

SOUND AND TOUGH
The best Anglo-arabs have strong limbs and feet that are able to withstand hard work.

DEEP GIRTH
The Thoroughbred should have a deep girth. This allows for its lungs to expand fully when the horse is galloping.

Born to race

The Thoroughbred is built for speed. There are two different types. Flat racehorses are usually more finely built and race as two and three-year-olds. Steeplechasers race over fences and do not start until they are four years old. Their racing careers last much longer than flat racehorses, sometimes until they are about 13 years old.

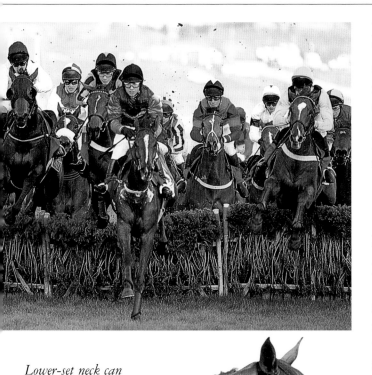

American Standardbred

The Standardbred is America's own racing breed. Its breeding has Thoroughbred influence from the 18th century. It is a harness racer that pulls a special lightweight vehicle, usually over distances of one mile (1.6 km). The breed's name comes from the 19th century, when horses had to meet a standard time in races to enter the breed register.

Lower-set neck can be stretched out in a racing finish.

POWERFUL QUARTERS
The Standardbred's croup is usually higher than its withers. This gives powerful thrust to the quarters, making the horse a successful harness racer.

Colors are mainly bay (as here) brown, black, and chestnut.

Strong limbs reduce the risk of injury when the horse is racing at speed.

AMERICAN STANDARDBRED

MOUNTAIN AND MOORLAND PONIES

MOUNTAIN AND MOORLAND ponies are able to survive harsh living conditions. They first came from the British Isles, where they are native ponies, but are now bred all over the world. They can carry heavy weights for their size, and the larger breeds can be ridden by adults or children. They are often crossed with Thoroughbreds to produce sport horses.

Moorland ponies
The Exmoor is a rare breed. It has a fan of hair at the top of the tail, called an ice tail, which protects it from bad weather. Another moorland pony, the Dartmoor pony, is more elegant than the Exmoor.

Exmoors are always bay, brown, or dun.

Small breeds
Dartmoor, Exmoor, Shetland, and Welsh A and B ponies are small but strong. Their kind temperaments and athletic abilities make them good to ride if trained correctly. They are also suitable for driving.

Double-layered coat in winter protects pony from harsh weather.

Head has intelligent expression and small pointed ears.

WELSH SECTION A

Neck is not too long and is slightly arched.

This breed can be any color except pinto.

Bodies should be strong and deep.

Tough hooves mean they do not always need shoes.

Short cannons

SHETLAND
The Shetland is the smallest British native pony breed, and originated from the bleak Shetland Islands off the coast of Scotland. Its average height is 40 in (1 m), and it is the only breed that is not measured in hands.

WELSH PONIES
The Welsh Section A, or Welsh Mountain pony, is particularly well proportioned and elegant. The Section B, or Welsh pony, is slightly stockier.

Large breeds

The larger British ponies are bred as performance ponies for children and adults. The Connemara and Welsh Section D are the most popular and are often good jumpers.

Long neck and good shoulder make a comfortable ride.

Usual colors are bay, brown, and chestnut.

Strong hocks and hindquarters for powerful stride.

Connemara is usually gray, dun, or bay.

NEW FOREST
New Forest ponies have been influenced by the introduction of Welsh and Thoroughbred blood. They are sure-footed and have kind temperaments.

WELSH SECTION D
Also called the Welsh Cob, this pony is the largest British native breed and can be over 15 hh. It often has a powerful trot.

CONNEMARA
Originally bred in Ireland and popular throughout the world, the Connemara has a range of uses, from dressage to jumping.

Strong back and hindquarters for carrying weight

FELL

Tails and manes are uncut.

Coat is usually dun or gray in color.

Fine, silky feathers on lower legs

FELL AND DALES
The Fell and Dales ponies look similar, although the Fell is slightly smaller and lighter in build. Both are usually black, brown, or bay and have thick, silky leg feathers.

HIGHLAND
The Highland pony is very strong and can carry a weight of up to 278 lb (126 kg). It often has a dark stripe, called an eel stripe, down the center of its back.

EUROPEAN PONIES

EUROPEAN PONIES might not be as well known worldwide as British ponies, but their popularity is growing fast. Haflingers and Norwegian Fjords, in particular, make good riding and driving ponies, and are prized as purebreds rather than as possible crosses with Thoroughbreds. The Haflinger has influenced the Italian Bardigiano, while the Norwegian Fjord resembles the Highland pony.

Bardigiano

The Bardigiano is an Italian breed of mountain pony. It has been influenced by draft horse blood and by the Avelignese, a pony that is very similar to, but heavier than, the Haflinger.

Coat is often bay or brown, with no white markings.

Pony power

Many European ponies are kept for work as well as for pleasure. They are usually strong and sturdy, which makes them ideal for harness work in mountainous areas. They also thrive in harsh conditions, and are less expensive to feed than large horses.

Mane is cut to stand on end, so the black center shows through.

A straight, rather than sloping, shoulder and flat withers make it difficult to fit a saddle.

FJORD
The Norwegian Fjord looks in many ways like its ancestor, the Asiatic Wild horse. It is always dun in color and is about 13 to 14 hh.

Stripes or zebra bars are common on legs.

The Piebald Pottok stands up to 13 hh.

A straight back and flat withers are common characteristics.

The shape of the legs is improved by Welsh Section B and Arabian blood.

Brown, black, bay, and liver chestnut, often with white markings on the head, are the most common colors.

POTTOK
The Pottok is a semiwild pony from the Basque region of France. There are three types: the Standard, the Piebald (Pinto), and the Double.

LANDAIS
The Landais is an established French pony breed with Welsh and Arabian influence. It is hardy and willing, and stands between about 11 and 13.2 hh.

Thick, flaxen mane, like tail

Open nostrils for easy breathing in oxygen-poor mountain air

HAFLINGER
The Austrian Haflinger is always chestnut or palomino and ranges from 13.2 to 15 hh. It is the most attractive and adaptable of the European breeds.

SNOW PONIES
Sleighs pulled by Haflingers are a special attraction in the Austrian mountains. Ponies are not put in a harness until they are four years old, and many work until they are about 30.

PONIES WORLDWIDE

ALL PONIES AND horses are bred to carry out specific tasks. As the type of work ponies are bred for changes, so do the qualities and characteristics that breeders aim for. This has led to the creation of new breeds, such as the Pony of the Americas, and miniature breeds, such as the Falabella. Some breeds, such as the Caspian, are kept for riding; others, such as the American Shetland, are used for driving; and some, like the Bashkir, even provide milk.

Pony of the Americas
The Pony of the Americas was first bred in 1954 and is a cross between a Shetland and an Appaloosa. It is now a recognized breed, prized for its spotted coat and its suitability as a riding pony.

The pony's height is set between 11.2 and 13.2 hh.

Small and beautiful
Falabellas and miniature Shetlands are bred to be as small as possible. They are too small to be ridden, and some people believe that this is wrong. There is certainly a danger that breeding to create a small animal increases the risk of weakness, such as loss of strength and a poor constitution.

Back is straight and tail carried high.

Perfectly proportioned head

FALABELLA
The Falabella takes its name from an Argentinian family that developed the breed. It is really a horse but is never more than 30 in (76 cm) tall and it is sometimes called a pony.

Luxurious tail growth, like mane

Fine coat offers little protection against harsh weather.

CASPIAN
The Caspian is probably a forerunner of the Arabian horse. It is an elegant riding pony, suitable for small children, and it stands between 10 and 12 hh.

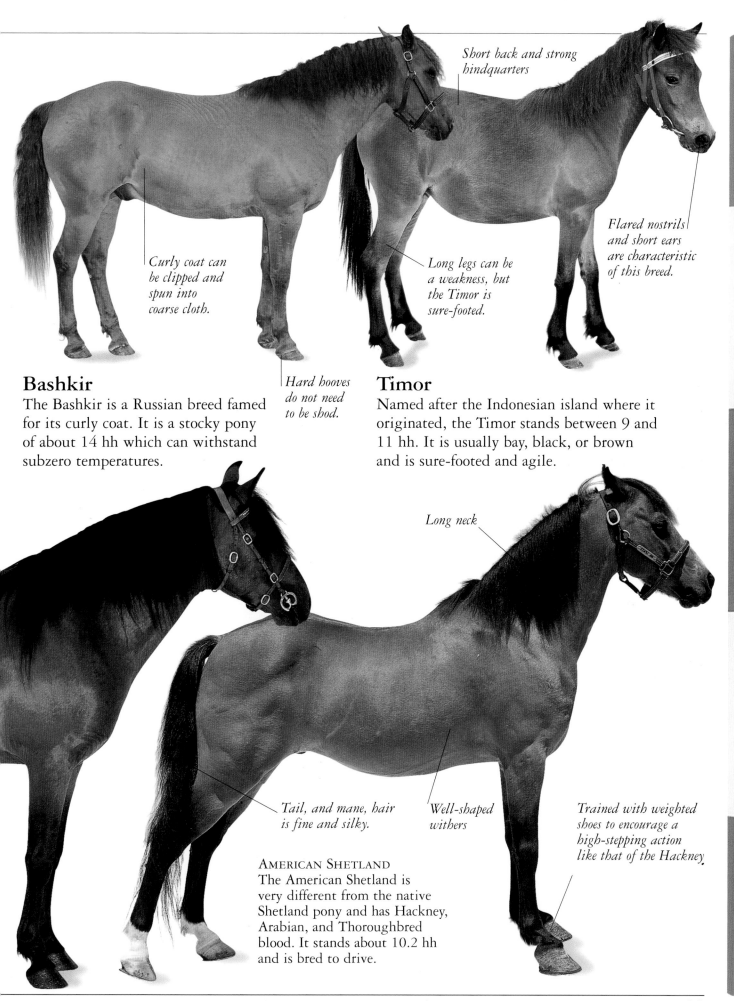

Short back and strong hindquarters

Flared nostrils and short ears are characteristic of this breed.

Curly coat can be clipped and spun into coarse cloth.

Long legs can be a weakness, but the Timor is sure-footed.

Hard hooves do not need to be shod.

Bashkir

The Bashkir is a Russian breed famed for its curly coat. It is a stocky pony of about 14 hh which can withstand subzero temperatures.

Timor

Named after the Indonesian island where it originated, the Timor stands between 9 and 11 hh. It is usually bay, black, or brown and is sure-footed and agile.

Long neck

Tail, and mane, hair is fine and silky.

Well-shaped withers

Trained with weighted shoes to encourage a high-stepping action like that of the Hackney.

AMERICAN SHETLAND
The American Shetland is very different from the native Shetland pony and has Hackney, Arabian, and Thoroughbred blood. It stands about 10.2 hh and is bred to drive.

WARMBLOODS

THE TERM *warmblood* describes horses that are a mixture of either Thoroughbred or Arabian and other breeds. It is also used for European sport horses that have Thoroughbred influence but have been carefully bred. Warmbloods are graded for athleticism, soundness, and good conformation. They now dominate international dressage and show jumping.

Hanoverian

The Hanoverian is the best-known warmblood. Its ancestry can be traced back to 1735 at Celle in Germany. This breed was originally heavier than those today, which have a greater percentage of Thoroughbred blood to give them power and elegance.

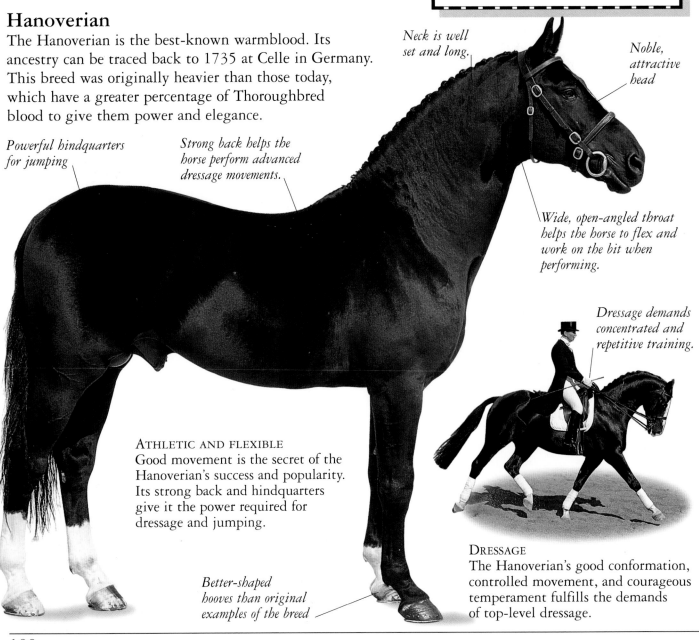

Powerful hindquarters for jumping

Strong back helps the horse perform advanced dressage movements.

Neck is well set and long.

Noble, attractive head

Wide, open-angled throat helps the horse to flex and work on the bit when performing.

Dressage demands concentrated and repetitive training.

ATHLETIC AND FLEXIBLE
Good movement is the secret of the Hanoverian's success and popularity. Its strong back and hindquarters give it the power required for dressage and jumping.

Better-shaped hooves than original examples of the breed

DRESSAGE
The Hanoverian's good conformation, controlled movement, and courageous temperament fulfills the demands of top-level dressage.

Back length is in perfect proportion.

Withers and neck angles are ideal for a riding horse.

Thoroughbred blood has improved back conformation.

Powerful shoulders for jumping

Good hooves and forelegs

Danish warmblood

Denmark's sport horse has been developed over the past 30 years by crossing the Frederiksborg, a Danish carriage horse, with Thoroughbred and Thoroughbred crosses. The Danish warmblood is more elegant than the Hanoverian and is renowned for its kind nature.

Dutch warmblood

The Dutch warmblood is a combination of the Gelderlander, a carriage horse breed, the heavy Groningen, and the Thoroughbred. It excels in both show jumping and dressage. Mated with Thoroughbred mares, it produces elegant but powerful offspring.

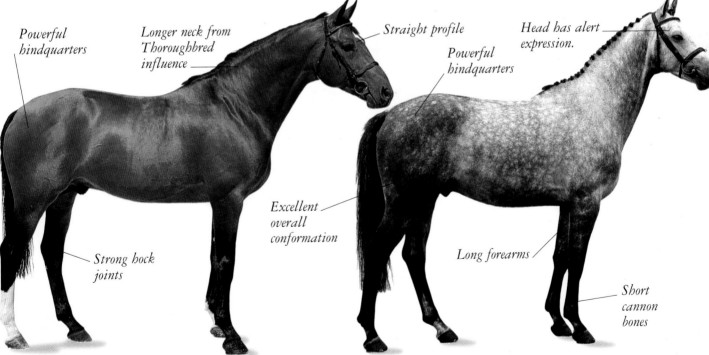

Powerful hindquarters

Longer neck from Thoroughbred influence

Strong hock joints

Straight profile

Powerful hindquarters

Excellent overall conformation

Head has alert expression.

Long forearms

Short cannon bones

Selle Français

France's warmblood is unique in that its ancestry is with the trotting horse. It has been refined by Thoroughbred and Anglo-Arab blood. The result is a horse that excels mainly at jumping, but has the speed and agility for eventing.

Trakehner

The Trakehner originated in East Prussia, now part of Poland, and is a model of the ideal competition horse. Its combined elegance, substantial frame, and courageous and willing temperament allow it to excel in all areas.

IRISH DRAFT AND CLEVELAND BAY

THE IRISH DRAFT and Cleveland Bay were originally bred to pull carts rather than to be ridden. Today these breeds are mainly crossed with Thoroughbreds to produce competition horses. The Irish Draft is a particularly popular influence on horses bred for show jumping and eventing.

TALENT FOR JUMPING
Irish Draft blood breeds many talented show jumpers. Great strength in the hindquarters, agility, and boldness are its hallmarks.

Irish Draft

The Irish Draft is deep-bodied with good legs. Bred for agricultural work, it was also expected to carry Irish farmers out hunting. This helped to develop an athletic, sure-footed horse.

Neck length in proportion to body

Tail is black, as is the mane.

Strong hind legs and quarters for jumping

Deep girth helps maintain stamina.

Deep chest and a sloping shoulder give strength and good length of stride.

Black lower legs

SPORT HORSE
The modern Irish Draft is crossed with the English Thoroughbred to produce a sport horse conformation. It is now longer in the neck and less likely to have flat hooves than the older type of Irish Draft.

Large hooves that can be too low in the heel

Bavarian warmblood

The Cleveland Bay has had a strong influence on the Bavarian warmblood, one of the lesser-known warmblood sport horses. In the 18th century, half-bred Cleveland Bay stallions were imported to Bavaria to give greater substance to the horses bred there.

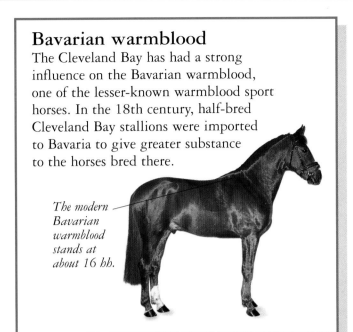

The modern Bavarian warmblood stands at about 16 hh.

CARRIAGE HORSES
The Cleveland Bay has always been a royal carriage horse in the UK, and is still kept by the royal family. Cleveland stock has been sent all over the world, particularly to the US.

Cleveland Bay

This breed is always bay with black points (mane, tail, ear tips, and lower legs). Its head is said to show influence from the Andalusian.

Broad between the eyes

Large head

Slender neck

Deep through girth

CHANGING TIMES
The original Cleveland Bay had upright legs and shoulders for pulling power. Now popular as a cross for riding horses, it is bred with a more sloping shoulder and less upright pasterns. This gives a more comfortable action for riding.

Good, hard hooves

CLEVELAND BAY

- Good jumper and hunter and a superb carriage horse

- One of the longest-living of all the breeds, up to about 30 years

- Especially powerful in neck and through shoulder

- Always bay with black points

- Most stand between 16 and 16.2hh

- Clean legs without feathers

- Has a hardy constitution plus stamina and strength

HEAVY HORSES

HEAVY HORSES are the giants of the horse world. Bred to work on the land and to pull heavy loads, they are usually not less than 16.2 hh and often reach heights in excess of 17 hh. The oldest heavy horse breed is probably the Ardennes from France and Belgium, which can be traced back more than 2,000 years. The Shire is the best-known heavy horse and is descended from the medieval war horse.

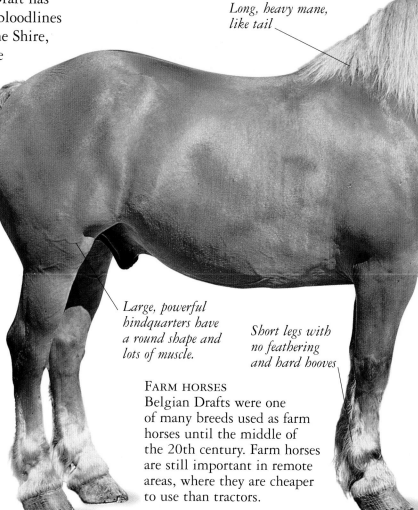

Thick mane

Percherons are often dapple gray.

Percheron

The Percheron is the lightest of the heavy horses, but it is still very powerful. It has no feathering and is prized for its calm and pleasant temperament.

Belgian Draft

Also known as the Brabant, the Belgian Draft has had a great influence on other breeds. Its bloodlines have contributed to the development of the Shire, the Clydesdale, the Suffolk Punch, and the Irish Draft. It is bred mainly in Belgium but is popular in the US.

Long, heavy mane, like tail

Tail is traditionally tied up for work.

Funeral horses

The Friesian is the lightest of the coldblooded breeds. It is mainly a harness horse and is popular for pulling hearses because of its black coat. The Friesian can be ridden and has a energetic trot.

The Friesian stands 15 hh and upward.

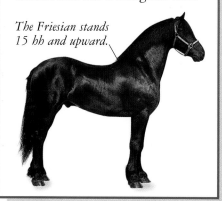

Large, powerful hindquarters have a round shape and lots of muscle.

Short legs with no feathering and hard hooves

FARM HORSES
Belgian Drafts were one of many breeds used as farm horses until the middle of the 20th century. Farm horses are still important in remote areas, where they are cheaper to use than tractors.

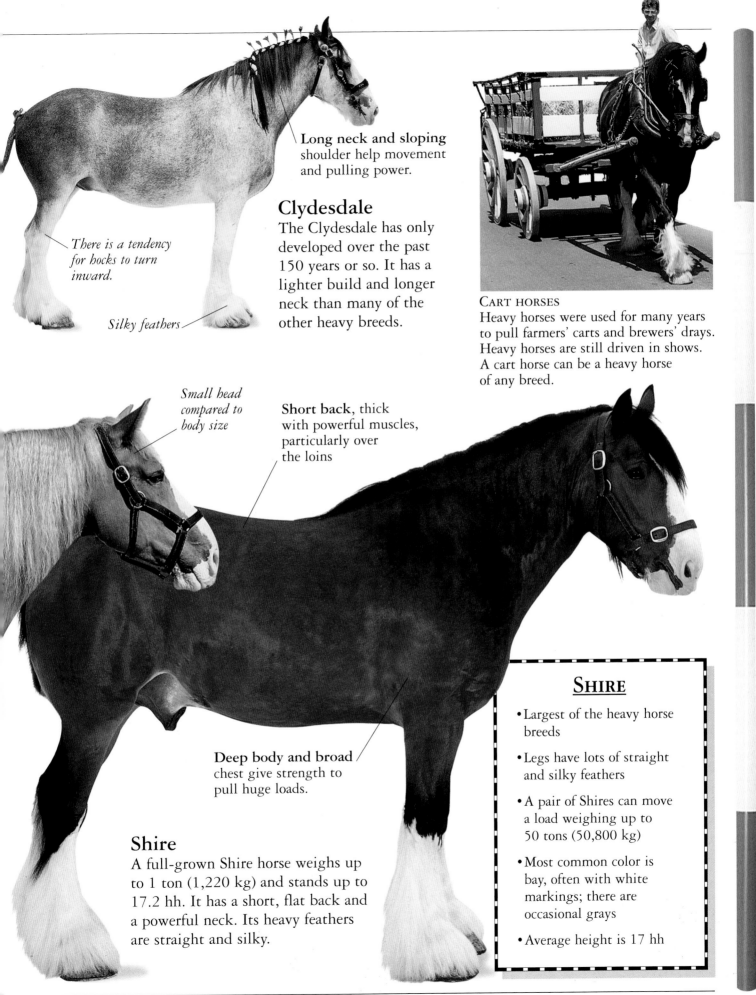

Long neck and sloping shoulder help movement and pulling power.

Clydesdale
The Clydesdale has only developed over the past 150 years or so. It has a lighter build and longer neck than many of the other heavy breeds.

There is a tendency for hocks to turn inward.

Silky feathers

CART HORSES
Heavy horses were used for many years to pull farmers' carts and brewers' drays. Heavy horses are still driven in shows. A cart horse can be a heavy horse of any breed.

Small head compared to body size

Short back, thick with powerful muscles, particularly over the loins

Deep body and broad chest give strength to pull huge loads.

Shire
A full-grown Shire horse weighs up to 1 ton (1,220 kg) and stands up to 17.2 hh. It has a short, flat back and a powerful neck. Its heavy feathers are straight and silky.

SHIRE
- Largest of the heavy horse breeds
- Legs have lots of straight and silky feathers
- A pair of Shires can move a load weighing up to 50 tons (50,800 kg)
- Most common color is bay, often with white markings; there are occasional grays
- Average height is 17 hh

PRIZED FOR COLOR

MANY HORSES are popular because of their coat colors. They include Paints, Pintos, Appaloosas, and Palominos. Some, such as Appaloosas, are classed as breeds, while others, such as Pintos, are types. In some breeds and types the color and pattern of the coat is always the same.

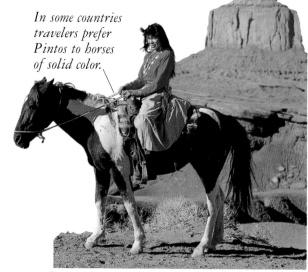

In some countries travelers prefer Pintos to horses of solid color.

PAINTS
Paints are either overo or tobiano, depending on where and how much white is in their coats. Paints were prized by the Native Americans.

Spotted horses

Appaloosas are often called spotted horses. There are also spotted ponies. The American Appaloosa was developed by the Nez Percé Indians in the 18th century. The Pony of the Americas is a cross between the Appaloosa and the Shetland.

Mane, like tail, is usually sparse and short.

Sclera (white ring) around eyes is feature of an Appaloosa.

Skin on nose and nostrils is often mottled.

Deep through the girth with a strong back

Long forearms help good movement.

Cannon bones should be short.

APPALOOSA
The Appaloosa is a sport horse and should have athletic conformation. It is usually about 15.2 hh. The American Appaloosa often contains some Quarter Horse blood.

Good, hard hooves allow some Appaloosas to work unshod.

Hooves often have vertical black and white stripes.

Colors not breeds

In most countries, horses such as Pintos and Palominos differ widely in build, from elegant riding horses to cobs and draft animals. They are therefore classed as types, not breeds. In the US, many horses of specific color are bred to a particular type and are classed as breeds.

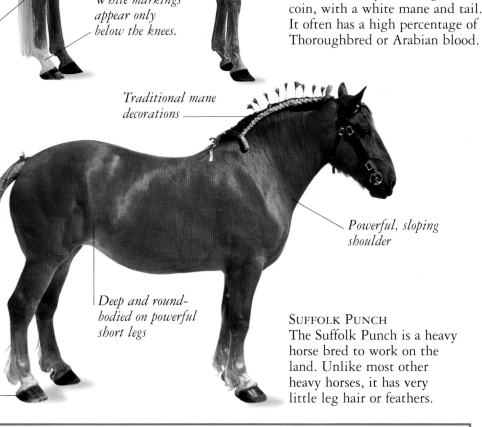

A Palomino's coat contains less than 15 percent dark hairs.

Arabian influence is often noticeable in tail.

White markings appear only below the knees.

PALOMINO
The perfect Palomino is the color of a newly minted gold coin, with a white mane and tail. It often has a high percentage of Thoroughbred or Arabian blood.

Breed colors

Suffolk Punches and Cleveland Bays are always the same color. The Cleveland Bay is always bay, and the Suffolk Punch is always one of seven shades of chestnut. If either breed is crossed with a Thoroughbred, the color is often, but not always, passed on.

Traditional mane decorations

Powerful, sloping shoulder

Deep and round-bodied on powerful short legs

Round, hard hooves are smaller than many heavy breeds.

SUFFOLK PUNCH
The Suffolk Punch is a heavy horse bred to work on the land. Unlike most other heavy horses, it has very little leg hair or feathers.

Pattern variations

Appaloosas and Paints both have a number of recognized coat patterns. Appaloosas are either leopard, blanket, snowflake, marble, or frost. Leopards have white backs and hips with dark spots. White blankets are white over the hips. Snowflakes have widespread dark spots, marbles have mottled body coloring, and frosts have dark coats with white flecks. The coat of a Paint is always a combination of white with another color. No two coat patterns are exactly alike, although markings may be similar within families.

LEOPARD PATTERN

Leopard pattern has large, dark spots.

Marbled pattern is mottled all over body.

MARBLE PATTERN

GAITED HORSES

MOST HORSES and ponies have four natural gaits: walk, trot, canter, and gallop. However, some breeds have special gaits and are known as gaited horses. These gaits make the horses particularly comfortable to ride or look spectacular in harness. A gait is a natural characteristic of a particular breed but may be encouraged and exaggerated with special training.

Traditionally shown with long, flowing manes and tails

COMFORTABLE RIDE
Tennessee Walking Horses are said to be the most comfortable of all riding horses. The breed is calm and kind, which makes it suitable for beginner and experienced riders alike.

Tennessee Walking Horse

The Tennessee Walking Horse originated in the southern states of the US and has Spanish ancestry. This breed looks quite ordinary when standing still, but its smooth, gliding gaits make it look very special when moving. It has three gaits: a flat or ordinary walk, a running walk, and a rocking horse canter.

Long, elegant neck helps horse balance.

Low head carriage

Long, sloping shoulder makes the horse comfortable to ride.

Black and chestnut are the most prevalent colors for show horses.

Coat can be any color, but solid colors are seen most often.

Hind hooves have long heels to accentuate the smooth action of the gaits.

Front hooves are deliberately kept longer than usual. Shoes may be lightly weighted to exaggerate the action of the gaits.

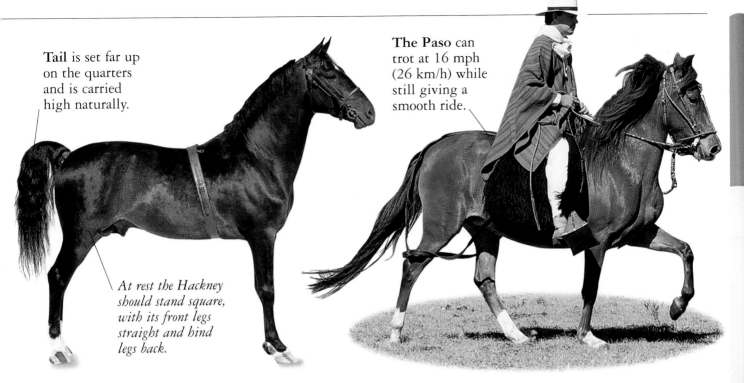

Tail is set far up on the quarters and is carried high naturally.

At rest the Hackney should stand square, with its front legs straight and hind legs back.

The Paso can trot at 16 mph (26 km/h) while still giving a smooth ride.

Hackney

The high-stepping Hackney is famous for its flamboyant trot. It is uncomfortable to ride, but makes a spectacular driving horse. There are Hackney ponies, which stand up to 14 hh, and Hackney horses, which reach about 15.3 hh.

Peruvian Paso

The Paso is descended from horses brought to Peru by 16th-century Spanish explorers. The Paso can canter, but is best known for its trot. Its three trots are called Paso Corto, Paso Fino, and Paso Largo; ordinary, slow, and fast.

Short, stocky body on strong legs carries heavy weights.

There are 15 recognized colors, although pinto and palomino are rare.

Icelandics are often chestnut with flaxen mane and tail.

Tolt is an effortless pace that can be kept up for long distances.

Hooves are hard and tough, which improves agility in crossing rough country.

Icelandic horse

Although the Icelandic horse never stands more than 13.2 hh and is often smaller, it is always called a horse and never a pony. It is very strong for its size and is ridden by adults, even in races.

TOLT

The Icelandic horse has five natural gaits. The most famous is the tolt, a running walk that is used to cross uneven ground at high speed.

HORSES FOR HERDSMEN

HORSES AND HERDSMEN have always been natural partners. A rider on a trained horse can herd sheep, cattle, and even other horses, while people on foot or in motor vehicles would fail. Some breeds, such as the Camargue horse and the Quarter Horse, have been developed especially for herding. A good herdsman's horse is fast and agile and learns to anticipate its rider's next command.

Rounding up sheep

Wherever sheep are kept, horses and ponies are used to move them from one place to another. The Australian Stock horse, Exmoor pony, and Welsh Cob are all perfect for this type of work.

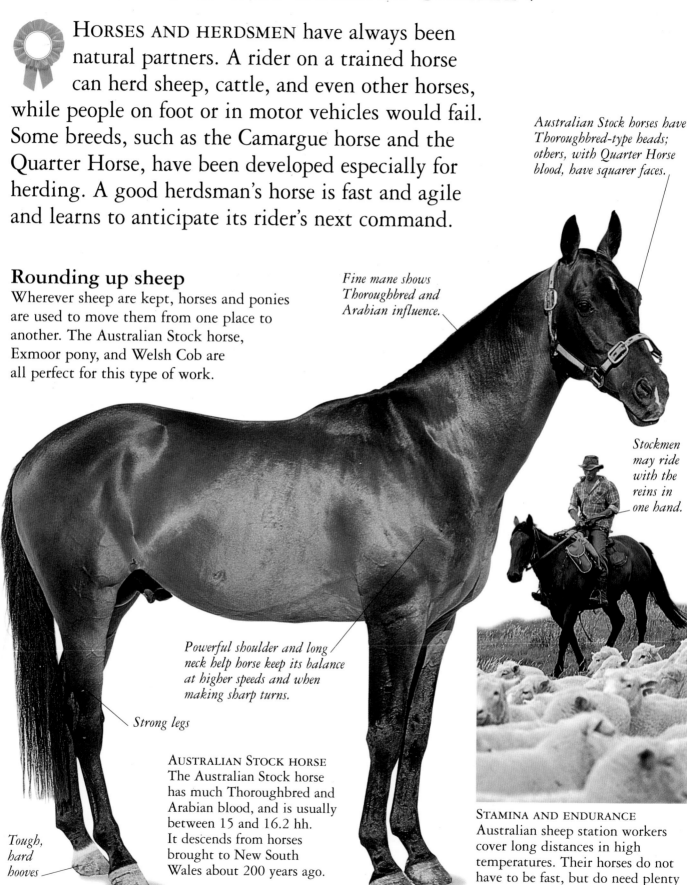

Australian Stock horses have Thoroughbred-type heads; others, with Quarter Horse blood, have squarer faces.

Fine mane shows Thoroughbred and Arabian influence.

Stockmen may ride with the reins in one hand.

Powerful shoulder and long neck help horse keep its balance at higher speeds and when making sharp turns.

Strong legs

AUSTRALIAN STOCK HORSE
The Australian Stock horse has much Thoroughbred and Arabian blood, and is usually between 15 and 16.2 hh. It descends from horses brought to New South Wales about 200 years ago.

Tough, hard hooves

STAMINA AND ENDURANCE
Australian sheep station workers cover long distances in high temperatures. Their horses do not have to be fast, but do need plenty of stamina and great endurance.

Work and play

The early American settlers used their cattle horses in harness and for entertainment. The favorite sports were sprint races over short distances and cattle-cutting competitions.

Muscular hindquarters for turning power

CUTTING HORSES
A herd rider often has to single out one cow or calf from the rest of the herd. Many good cutting horses are Quarter Horses and they are highly prized for their abilities.

QUARTER HORSE
The Quarter Horse was used for work and sport. It was traditionally raced over a quarter of a mile, which is how it got its name.

Joints must be strong to take stress of sharp turns and halts.

Herding cows

In some parts of France, the US, Australia, and other countries, horses are still used to round up cattle. The Camargue horses bred in France herd wild black bulls, which can be fierce and aggressive.

Thick tail for protection against flies

Halters made from twisted horsehair are traditionally worn by Camargue horses.

CAMARGUE HORSE
Although the Camargue horse only stands between 13.2 and 14.2 hh, it is always called a horse rather than a pony and is very powerful. Camargue horses have lived in the Rhône delta for over a thousand years.

RIDE 'EM, COWBOY!
Although there are few true cowboys today, some horses are still used to round up cattle. Cowboys need horses that are both intelligent and well trained.

WILD HORSES

TODAY THERE IS only one truly wild horse – Przewalski's Horse. However, there are many other types and breeds, such as Mustangs from the western US and Brumbies from Australia, that are often called wild but are in fact feral. These horses have ancestors that were domesticated but later escaped into the wild, where they formed herds. Wild and feral horses have to survive on poor-quality and often scarce grazing.

Stallions will fight others if provoked.

RUNNING WILD
Horse herds consist of mares, foals, and young horses. Each herd is led by a stallion, which defends the territory, and there is also a lead mare that dominates the other mares.

Feral horses
Wild and feral horses are often resented by farmers because they graze on land needed for livestock. Mustangs are protected by law in the US and some are caught and domesticated to safeguard the future of the breed.

Some Mustangs have dark stripes, called eel stripes, that run down their backs.

MUSTANG
The Mustang is descended from the Spanish horse and its name comes from a Spanish word, *mestena*, which means a herd of horses. The Mustang was the foundation for many of the American breeds and has retained many Spanish characteristics, especially its color.

Hard hooves are essential for survival when covering large areas of land.

Zebras and donkeys
Zebras and donkeys belong to the same family as the horse. All are related to *Pliohippus*, the first horse ancestor to run on one toe. The African wild ass is the relative of the domesticated donkey. There are several different species of zebras, including the common zebra, and Grevy's zebra.

Every zebra has a unique striped pattern.

A donkey when crossed with a horse produces a mule.

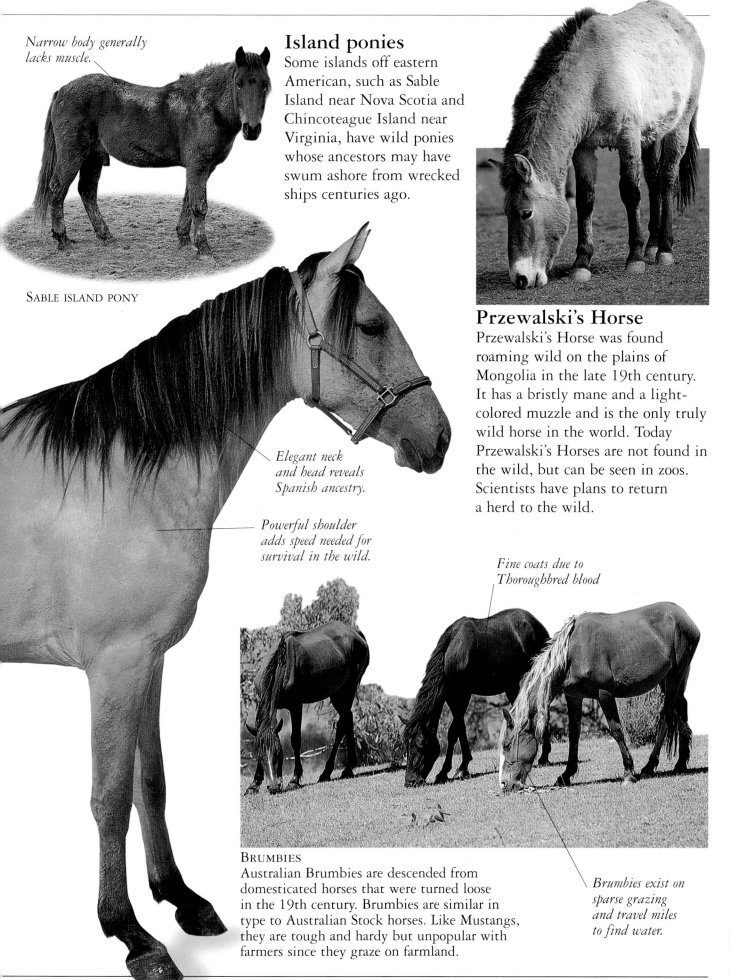

Narrow body generally lacks muscle.

SABLE ISLAND PONY

Island ponies
Some islands off eastern American, such as Sable Island near Nova Scotia and Chincoteague Island near Virginia, have wild ponies whose ancestors may have swum ashore from wrecked ships centuries ago.

Przewalski's Horse
Przewalski's Horse was found roaming wild on the plains of Mongolia in the late 19th century. It has a bristly mane and a light-colored muzzle and is the only truly wild horse in the world. Today Przewalski's Horses are not found in the wild, but can be seen in zoos. Scientists have plans to return a herd to the wild.

Elegant neck and head reveals Spanish ancestry.

Powerful shoulder adds speed needed for survival in the wild.

Fine coats due to Thoroughbred blood

BRUMBIES
Australian Brumbies are descended from domesticated horses that were turned loose in the 19th century. Brumbies are similar in type to Australian Stock horses. Like Mustangs, they are tough and hardy but unpopular with farmers since they graze on farmland.

Brumbies exist on sparse grazing and travel miles to find water.

HORSE AND PONY CHART

This chart gives you an overall view of all the horses and ponies mentioned in this book. Use it as a quick-reference guide to look up the differences between each breed or type.

TYPES

COB	HUNTER	HUNTER	POLO PONY	RIDING HORSE
• Any color, usually gray • Up to 15.3 hh • Riding and driving		• Any color • Around 16 – 16.2 hh • Hunting	• Any color • Around 15.1 hh • Polo matches	• Any color • Up to 15 – 16.2 hh • All types of riding

LIGHT

ANDALUSIAN	ANGLO-ARAB	APPALOOSA	APPALOOSA	ARABIAN
• Bay, shades of gray, mulberry • Around 15.2 hh • Dressage, parade riding	• Chestnut, bay, brown • 15 – 16.3 hh • All riding sports	• Black, brown, chestnut and white • 14.2 – 15.2 hh • Western riding, all sports		• Any solid color • 14.2 – 15 hh • Endurance, racing
AUSTRALIAN STOCK • Any solid color • 15 – 16.2 hh • Herding sheep and cattle, general riding	BAVARIAN WARMBLOOD • Any solid color • Around 16 hh • All sports	CLEVELAND BAY • Bay • 16 – 16.2 hh • Riding, driving		DANISH WARMBLOOD • Any solid color • 16.1 – 16.2 hh • Dressage, show jumping
DUTCH WARMBLOOD • Any color, bay and brown most common • 15.2 – 16.2 hh • Show jumping, dressage	HACKNEY • Dark brown, black, bay, chestnut • 15 – 15.3 hh • Driving	HANOVERIAN • Any solid color • 15.3 – 16.2 hh • Dressage, show jumping	ICELANDIC HORSE • Chestnut, dun, bay, gray, black • 12.3 – 13.2 hh • Riding, all sports	IRISH DRAFT • Any solid color • 15.2 – 17 hh • Show jumping, all riding, hunting
LIPIZZAN • Gray • 15.1 – 16.2 hh • Dressage, driving	LUSITANO • Any color, mainly gray • 15 – 16 hh • Dressage	PERUVIAN PASO • Any color, mainly bay and chestnut • 14 – 15 hh • Riding	QUARTER HORSE • Any solid color, mainly chestnut • 14.3 – 16 hh • Riding, racing, herding, cutting	SELLE FRANCAIS • Any color, mainly chestnut • 15.2 – 16.2 hh • Dressage, eventing, show jumping
SHAGYA ARAB • Any solid color, mainly gray • Around 15 hh • Riding	STANDARDBRED • Any solid color • Around 15.2 hh • Harness racing, endurance	TENNESSEE WALKING • Black and solid colors • 15 – 16 hh • Riding	THOROUGHBRED • Any solid color • 15 – 16.2 hh • Racing, eventing	TRAKEHNER • Any solid colors • 16 – 16.2 hh • Dressage, show jumping

WILD AND FERAL

BRUMBIES	CAMARGUE	MUSTANG		PRZEWALSKI'S HORSE
• All colors • 15 – 16.2 hh • Australia	• Gray • 13.1 – 14.1 hh • France	• All colors • 13.2 – 15 hh • United States		• Dun • Around 14.3 hh • Mongolia

MUSTANG

HEAVY

BELGIAN DRAFT • Bay, dun, gray, red-roan • 16.2 – 17 hh • Farm work	**CLYDESDALE** • Bay, brown, gray, black, roan • 16.2 – 17 hh • Farm work	CLYDESDALE 	**FRIESIAN** • Black • Around 17 hh • Driving, riding
PERCHERON • Dapple-gray, black • 16 – 17 hh • Farm work	**SHIRE** • Black, bay, brown, gray • 16.2 – 17.2 hh • Farm work		**SUFFOLK PUNCH** • Shades of chesnut • 16 – 16.3 hh • Farm work

PONIES

AMERCAN SHETLAND • Brown, black, bay, chestnut, roan cream, dun, gray • 42 in (103 cm) • Driving	**BARDIGIANO** • Bay, brown • Up to 13.3 hh • Riding, farm work	**BASHKIR** • Red chestnut, bay, light brown • Around 14 hh • Riding, driving, kept for milk	**CASPIAN** • Bay, gray, chestnut, black, cream • 10 – 12 hh • Child's riding	**CONNEMARA** • Usually gray • 13 – 14.2 hh • Riding, driving
DARTMOOR • Bay, black, brown • Around 12.2 hh • Child's riding, driving	**DALES** • Black, bay, brown • Up to 14.2 hh • Farm work, trekking	**EXMOOR** • Bay, brown, dun • 12.2 – 12.3 hh • Riding	**FALABELLA** • Any color • 30 in (76 cm) • Pet only FALABELLA	
FELL • Black, brown, bay, gray • Up to 14 hh • Riding, driving	**NORWEGIAN FJORD** • Dun • 13 – 14 hh • Riding	**HAFLINGER** • Chestnut, palomino • Up to 13.3 hh • Driving	**HIGHLAND** • Dun, gray, brown, black, bay • Up to 14.2 hh • Riding, driving, packhorse	**LANDAIS** • Any color • 11.3 – 13.1 hh • Riding
 FELL / NEW FOREST		**NEW FOREST pony** • Any color except pinto • 14.2 hh • Riding, driving	**PONY OF THE AMERICAS** • Black, brown, chestnut and white • 11.2 – 13.2 hh • Child's riding	**POTTOK** • Any color • 11.1 – 14.2 hh • Riding, farm work
SHETLAND • Any color except pinto • 40 in (101 cm) • Child's riding, driving	**TIMOR** • Bay, black, brown • 9 – 11 hh • Riding, farm work	**WELSH SECTION A** • Any color except pinto • Up to 12 hh • Riding, driving		
WELSH SECTION B • Any color except pinto • Up to 13.2 hh • Riding, driving	**WELSH SECTION C** • Any color except pinto • 13.2 hh • Riding, driving, trekking	**WELSH SECTION D** • Any color except pinto • Over 13.2 hh • Riding, driving	POTTOK	

SHOWS &EVENTS

WHAT TO ENTER

WHATEVER SORT OF riding you enjoy, you can also compete. There are competitions at all levels to suit everyone from the beginner to the advanced rider, and from the novice horse to the experienced one. Everyone likes to win prizes, but competing is more than that. It allows you to monitor your progress and that of your horse, and have fun at the same time.

Horse and rider in harmony

Half pass is an advanced dressage movement.

Dressage
Dressage demonstrates the horse's balance and suppleness, the rider's skill, and the communication between horse and rider. Riders perform tests made up of a series of movements, which are judged for accuracy and harmony.

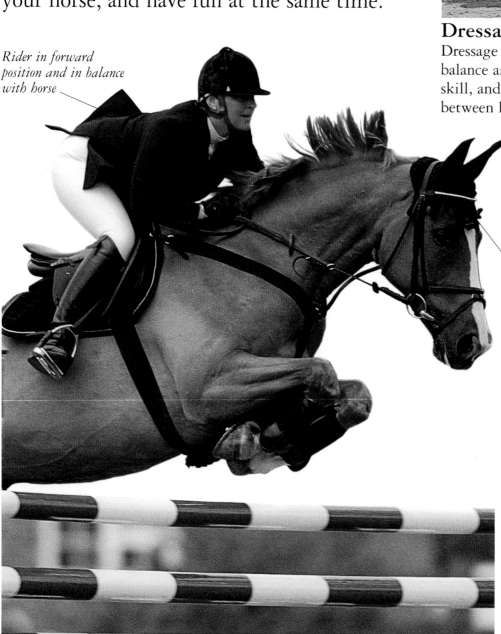

Rider in forward position and in balance with horse

Fly fringes are permitted in the show jumping ring for protection against flies.

Show jumping
Show jumpers need to be balanced and athletic. The riders' aim is to complete a course of fences without penalties for knockdowns or refusals, often against the clock. Puissance competitions have fewer fences and test how high a horse can jump. All horses and ponies can be taught to jump, but some have more natural talent for it than others.

Endurance

This is a fast-growing sport. There are local and international competitions that range from about 20 miles (32 km) to more than 100 miles (160 km). Many riders also take part in noncompetitive pleasure rides of 10–15 miles (16–24 km).

Showing

Showing classes are judged on a horse's or pony's conformation, movement, and ride. A good show horse or pony must be well schooled with good manners. Different countries have different types of show class. Equitation classes focus purely on the rider – the horse is not judged.

Eventing

Horse trials, or eventing, are the ultimate challenge. There are three phases – dressage, show jumping, and cross-country. Top-level three-day events include steeplechase, and roads and tracks phases. Horses must be calm and obedient for dressage, bold for cross-country, and balanced and careful for show jumping.

Top hats are only worn for formal occasions.

Black jacket adds to elegance.

GETTING FIT TO COMPETE

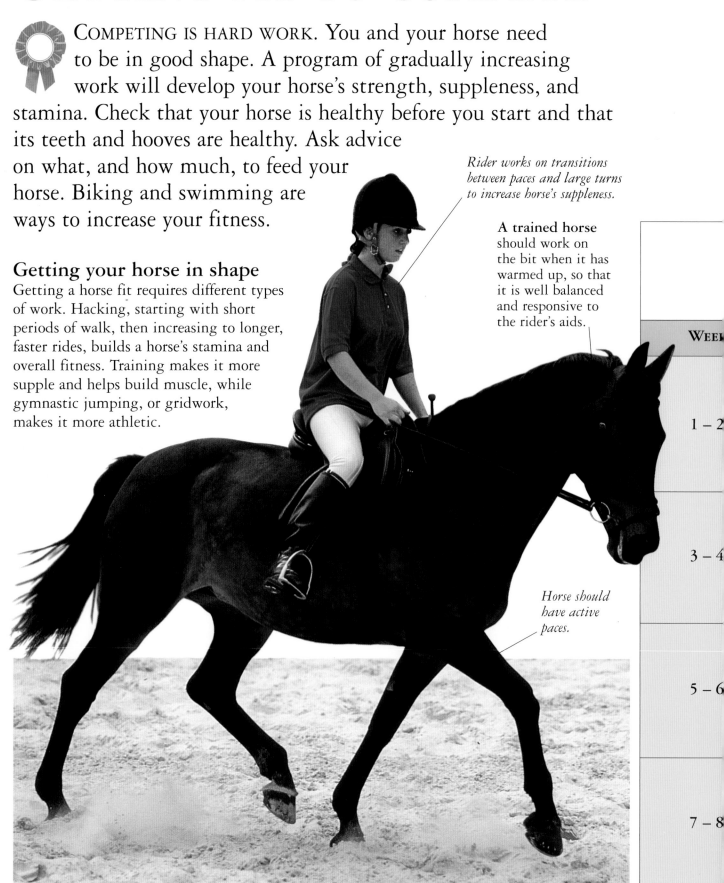

COMPETING IS HARD WORK. You and your horse need to be in good shape. A program of gradually increasing work will develop your horse's strength, suppleness, and stamina. Check that your horse is healthy before you start and that its teeth and hooves are healthy. Ask advice on what, and how much, to feed your horse. Biking and swimming are ways to increase your fitness.

Getting your horse in shape

Getting a horse fit requires different types of work. Hacking, starting with short periods of walk, then increasing to longer, faster rides, builds a horse's stamina and overall fitness. Training makes it more supple and helps build muscle, while gymnastic jumping, or gridwork, makes it more athletic.

Rider works on transitions between paces and large turns to increase horse's suppleness.

A trained horse should work on the bit when it has warmed up, so that it is well balanced and responsive to the rider's aids.

Horse should have active paces.

WEEK
1 – 2
3 – 4
5 – 6
7 – 8

HELP FROM OTHERS
If you have little time to ride your pony, knowledgeable parents or friends may be able to help. Lungeing is useful for ponies who are too small for adults; make sure your pony is not lunged more than three times a week, or it will get bored. When lungeing, work on both reins and increase the amount of work from 10 to 20 minutes.

Wear gloves when lungeing.

Side reins encourage pony to accept the bit.

EXERCISE ROUTINE

It is important to keep an exercise routine so you can judge the progress of your horse and spot potential problems. You must also feed correctly; balance forage (grass and hay) with hard feed (grain or pellets). Increase feed gradually; give more forage than hard feed.

ROADWORK	TRAINING & GRIDWORK	HACKING	FEED	CHECKLIST
Walk your horse on level ground for up to 20 minutes a day, building up to 45 minutes. Avoid any hill work.	*Walk should be active and balanced.*	Feed a horse on a ratio of 75–100% forage to 0–75% hard feed, such as grain or pellets.	If your horse is very unfit, extend the amount of walking exercise up to about six weeks.
Introduce short periods of working, rising trot. Do not work at sitting trot. Increase rides out by up to one hour.	Start to train for 15–20 minutes twice a week. Practice different exercises, such as large circles. Introduce canter in week four.	Trail ride four to five days a week. Introduce gradual hill work. Always walk downhill, but ride at a balanced trot uphill.	If in regular work, increase ratio of hard feed to 50%. *A scoop of grain*	Increase the amount of exercise a horse has before increasing its feed, not vice versa. Continue to turn your horse out daily to help it relax.
Basic work to strengthen tendons and ligaments now complete. Horse should have reached basic level of fitness.	Train at walk, trot, and canter three times a week, with short hacks if necessary.	When not training, take longer rides up to one-and-a-half hours. Ride up steep hills if possible.	If necessary, increase feed in line with horse's work.	Check horse's legs daily for signs of injury or lameness. Forage should not be less than 50% of diet for ponies and most horses.
Trotting poles help to improve balance.	Introduce gridwork as part of two training sessions a week. Gradually build up the heights and numbers of fences.	Continue with longer rides, including steep hills. Start fast work, but on ground that will not jar horse's hooves.	Increase feed to peak level, but continue to monitor horse's condition and reduce hard feed if horse is fit enough.	Check fit of saddle. A horse that builds muscle through training will continue to change shape.

CLOTHES AND TACK

CLOTHES AND TACK must be safe, comfortable and suitable for the horse and rider and the type of event they are entering. It is best to get expert advice on fitting tack, and to use equipment such as helmets and body protectors that meet the latest safety standards. Using damaged equipment increases the risk of accidents.

Safety helmet with chin strap

Riding jacket with shirt and tie

Beige jodhpurs

High-top leather boots

WHAT TO WEAR
This rider is dressed properly for general riding in competition. She could enter basic dressage, showing, and show jumping classes. Higher-level competition may require more formal clothes.

Special equipment
Different types of competitions require special equipment. Dressage, show jumping, horse trials, and Western classes all have rules about what the rider and horse should wear.

Safety helmets with colored silks are worn for eventing and long-distance riding.

Body protector helps prevent serious injury in the event of a fall.

Flash noseband prevents horse from opening its mouth, giving rider greater control.

Splint boots protect the horse on front and hind legs.

CROSS-COUNTRY CLOTHES
Jumping means that horse and rider need protective equipment. A rider may use different or additional tack, such as a breastplate for control.

Bell boots

SADDLES	BRIDLES

GENERAL-PURPOSE SADDLE

The general-purpose saddle is used for hacking (trail riding), flatwork, training, and jumping at basic levels. Advanced riders use special saddles for particular riding disciplines, but the general-purpose saddle is used by those who enjoy all types of riding.

Stirrup iron is secured by the stirrup leather.

GENERAL-PURPOSE SADDLE

SNAFFLE BRIDLE

This is the simplest bridle with one bit and one pair of reins. Novice riders should use this, and it should also be used when riding young horses. There are many designs of snaffle bits and nosebands.

Eggbutt snaffle

Reins

SNAFFLE BRIDLE

DRESSAGE SADDLE

This saddle is designed to make riding easier for the dressage rider, who rides with a longer, straighter leg. The saddle has straighter flaps and long girth straps, so that a short dressage girth can be used. Since there is less bulk under the dressage saddle, the horse is more responsive to the rider's leg aids.

DRESSAGE SADDLE

Long girth straps

DOUBLE BRIDLE

The double bridle has two bits and two pairs of reins that enable an expert dressage rider to give almost invisible aids or instructions. This bridle should only be used by expert riders on well-schooled horses. It is always used with a cavesson (plain noseband).

DOUBLE BRIDLE

Curb chain

Snaffle rein

Curb rein

JUMPING SADDLE

The forward-cut flaps of the jumping saddle make it easier for riders to ride with shorter stirrups. This helps to maintain a forward jumping position. Many riders use a general-purpose saddle for jumping courses up to 3 ft 3 in (1 m), but a jumping saddle is essential for bigger jumps.

Forward-cut design helps rider stay in balance.

JUMPING SADDLE

BOOTS

SPLINT BOOTS

Splint boots protect a horse's leg from blows, usually from another leg. Young, unbalanced horses and those that have poor movement should always wear boots. The boots can be used on the front and back legs.

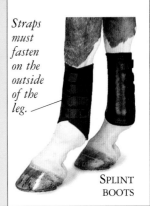

Straps must fasten on the outside of the leg.

SPLINT BOOTS

FOOT PROTECTORS	

BELL BOOTS

These boots are fitted around the lower part of the front legs (the pastern). They protect the horse from injury when it strikes the front heel with the toe of its hind foot. Horses may do this when galloping and jumping, or if they are unbalanced.

Bell boots fasten around the pastern.

BELL BOOTS

GALLOPING BOOTS

These boots protect the tendons on the front leg when struck by the horse's back legs. The boots are usually worn for galloping and jumping. Tendon injuries can weaken a horse for the rest of its life.

Boots fasten with clips, buckles, or Velcro.

GALLOPING BOOTS

GROOMED TO PERFECTION

SPECIAL GROOMING and braiding techniques make a horse look its best for competitions. A clean, shiny coat is essential, and braiding and quarter marks show off good conformation. Some breeds, such as Arabians, and Saddlebreds and Quarter Horses, are not shown with braided manes or tails.

QUARTER MARKS
Quarter marks show off the hindquarters. To make them, dampen the hair and make squares or diamonds by combing down against the lay of the hair. Alternatively, use a plastic template.

Quarter marks

Braiding the tail
Many people prefer braided tails to pulled ones, which have long side hairs pulled out. You can only braid a full tail. Take in just a few hairs at a time and keep your braid tight as you work down the tail.

Start right at the top and keep sections tight for neatness.

1 Dividing the hairs
Take small sections of hair from each side at the top of the tail. Cross the sections over and take a third from one side of the tail and bring it to the center.

Pass side sections over the center.

Keep hold of the center braid ends so that the whole braid remains tight.

2 Braid down the tail
Bring in small sections from each side and join them with the central braid. Braid down until the center braid reaches two-thirds of the way down the dock.

3 Loop braid under tail
Continue braiding without adding further hair. Loop the end under and stitch in place.

White socks and markings should be spotless.

Braiding the mane

A braided mane shows off a horse's neck. Pull or shorten the mane to about 5 in (12 cm) long before braiding, and thin it if necessary. Although rubber bands are quick to use, braids sewn with thread look neater and stay in place longer.

1 Divide mane into bunches

First dampen mane with water or hair gel. Then divide the mane into as many equal bunches as suits the length of the horse's neck. Fasten each bunch with a rubber band.

2 Braid down mane

Braid each bunch, keeping the braid tight so that short hairs stay in place. Double up the end hairs and fasten with a band or braiding thread that is the same color as the horse's mane.

3 Roll up braid on crest

If using thread, pass needle through top of braid. Roll braid up to the crest. Stitch the braids in place, or fasten them with rubber bands.

Some people use petroleum jelly for shine around eyes and mouth.

Whiskers may be trimmed for neatness.

Set braids on top of a thin neck and to the side of a heavy one.

A WELL-GROOMED HORSE Daily grooming helps maintain healthy skin and a shiny coat. Grease and dust dull the hair. If the weather is warm, you may want to bath your horse before a competition. A little coat gloss applied on a soft cloth adds extra shine for special occasions.

Take extra care when washing the tail of a green horse.

Hoof oil or polish should be used only for shows. Ask your farrier for advice on keeping hooves healthy.

Fetlock hair and hair around coronet neatly trimmed

Washing the tail

To wash a tail, stand to one side of the horse. Wet the hair, then work in a horse shampoo. Massage the top of the tail with your fingers to loosen grease or dirt, then work down the length of the tail. Rinse thoroughly and repeat if necessary. Squeeze out the water, then dry the tail by gently swishing it in circles.

PREPARING FOR A SHOW

START SHOW PREPARATION early; make sure your horse is ready and that your tack and equipment are in good condition. Your horse must be well shod and its vaccinations, or any other documents, must be up to date. Plan ahead; check when your class starts, then work out when you need to arrive at the show.

Preshow preparation

Prepare as much as possible the day before a show. Clean your tack, make sure your clothes are clean, and, if necessary, bathe your horse. You may want to braid your horse the day before if you have an early start. Make a list of things you need to take and get them ready in advance.

Hard hat and gloves

Black or blue show jacket

Stock with tie pin

High-top boots are usually worn by older riders. Younger riders normally wear jodhpur boots.

SHOW CLOTHES

For show classes or dressage wear a hard hat and gloves, and either a black or blue jacket with stock and stockpin, or a tweed jacket with shirt and tie. Choose beige breeches and long black boots or short jodhpur boots.

Leg wraps for horse

Bridle

Breastplate stops saddle from slipping

Long-sleeved shirt for cross-country events

Overgirth worn over saddle in cross-country events

Saddle with girth, stirrups, and leathers

Filled haynet

Water container

First-aid kit for horse

Water bucket

Tail guard to protect tail while traveling

Cell phone in case of emergency

Studs for shoes

Bell boots

First-aid kit for rider

Splint boots

Grooming kit

Cooler rug

Feed, if needed

Grease — use on horse's legs to help it slide over fences

High-top riding boots

Getting to the show

Allow plenty of time to load your horse and drive to the show. Make sure your horse wears protective traveling gear and a suitable blanket. Check that you have packed all the things you need for the day before loading your horse.

Ramps should have skid-proof surfaces and must be stable and level, to give the horse confidence as it walks up.

Look ahead and calmly lead horse up the ramp.

Leg wraps protect horse's legs while traveling.

Allow extra time for a young or inexperienced horse to settle when you arrive at the show.

Cover up your show clothes or change into them later.

THE TRAILER
Vehicles must be bright and inviting so the horse can see where it is going when loading. There must be enough headroom and each section inside the trailer must be wide enough for the size of horse.

Arrival

Try to arrive at the showgrounds an hour before your class starts. Check that your horse has not gotten hot or injured itself on the way to the show. Find out if classes are running on time, collect numbers, and make entries if necessary. Tack up and walk around until your horse settles down, then warm up lightly.

Stand to one side in case your horse kicks out in excitement.

BEFORE THE SHOW

- Check that horse is shod and its vaccinations are up to date

- Check that clothes and tack are clean and in good condition

- If you have an early start, bathe and braid horse day before show

- Check time of your class so you arrive at the show on time

YOUR FIRST SHOW

YOUR FIRST SHOW is likely to be a small, local competition with classes for novice horses and riders. These classes may include clear round jumping, equitation, pleasure, and trail classes. Shows with dressage tests at beginner level are also suitable. Do not enter more than two classes or your horse may become tired, especially if it is inexperienced.

If your horse is inexperienced you may just want to watch for the first time.

THE SHOWDESK
Go to the showdesk before your class starts, to register and receive your show number from an official. Check how many competitors there are before your turn, so you allow yourself time to warm up. Watch out for other riders in the practice ring, especially near practice jumps. Be ready to enter the show ring when called.

What to expect
At a show, you will see lots of horses, people, and vehicles, and you may hear loudspeaker announcements. Classes are held in areas called rings, and areas where people warm up are called practice rings. Show officials will give you a number to wear and they will tell you when it is your turn to compete.

If riding near parked horseboxes, watch out for other horses being unloaded.

Clear round jumping

Clear round jumping is a good introduction to show jumping for inexperienced horses and riders. You pay a small fee each time you attempt the course, and if you have problems, such as a refusal, you can try again. There is no jump-off, but usually each rider who jumps a clear round gets a special rosette. Think of it as a schooling round, not as a competition.

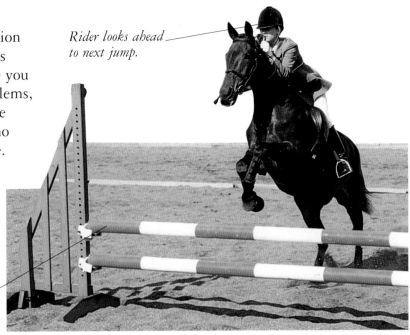

Rider looks ahead to next jump.

Clear round jumps are low, usually between 1 ft 6 in (45 cm) and 2 ft 6 in (75 cm). The jumps usually include small fillers and easy doubles.

ENJOYING YOUR SHOW

Shows should be fun for you and your horse. You may feel nervous at first, but concentrate on riding and caring for your horse correctly and you will soon feel more confident.

If something goes wrong, try not to panic. Keep calm, and remember that you will always have another chance, and that you and your horse will improve with practice.

	BEFORE THE SHOW	AT THE SHOW	IN THE RING	AFTER THE SHOW
PONY WELL-BEING	Allow plenty of time to load your horse into the trailer and to get to the show, so that both you and your horse are calm on arrival.	Do not ride your horse all day; get off and offer it water often. If your horse needs a feed, allow an hour for digestion before riding.	Stay calm if things go wrong. Do not panic or lose your temper – practicing at home will help you avoid problems next time.	Check that there are no minor injuries or loose shoes. Once back at home, your horse should be calm and comfortable, and not sweating.
HORSE AND RIDER SAFETY	Check that your tack, clothes, and other equipment are clean and in good repair. Horse's shoes must be secure and in good condition.	Beware of excitable horses – do not ride within kicking distance of other horses. Do not ride on pedestrian-only walkways.	Walk calmly into and out of the ring.	Clean tack, clothes, and any other equipment. Check all tack for breakages and send off for repair if necessary.
RIDER MANNERS (ETIQUETTE)	Thank those who have helped you get ready for the show, such as friends and the trailer driver. They will be happy to help you again.	Check in with ring official ten minutes before your turn. Use warm-up ring for your class and do not monopolize the practice fence.	Be courteous to other riders. Observe instructions given by officials. Acknowledge and thank judges where appropriate.	Do not criticise judges' decisions. Avoid temptation to leave muck from trailer at show-grounds. Take all refuse home.

GYMKHANAS

GYMKHANAS, or mounted games, are fast and fun. The word *gymkhana* originated in India; it means a meeting place for equestrian sports. Ponies are better at gymkhana games than horses because they are smaller and easier to turn and to vault onto. Riders have to be as quick and athletic as their ponies.

Mounted games

Balance and coordination are vital when taking part in mounted games. They can be played in teams or as individuals, and include bending races, in which riders have to ride in and out of a line of poles without touching any, and flag races, in which riders place flags in containers while on galloping ponies.

Tent pegging

Tent pegging is a military sport that began in India. An individual, or a team of four riders, carries a 10-ft (3-m) lance and gallops toward a row of tent pegs in the ground. The aim is to push the lance through the ring on the peg and lift it out without slowing down.

Fellow rider holds the pony with its reins in place, ready for the rider to vault on.

Speed and training

A good gymkhana pony has to be as well trained as a top polo pony. It must learn to twist and turn as the rider's body weight shifts, and to turn at top speed. It is important that you do not pull on the pony's mouth, so try to teach the pony to neck rein, so that it turns from the pressure of the reins against its neck, not pressure on its mouth.

Agility and obedience is important for mounted games. The pony needs to turn tightly around cones, while the rider needs to be equally agile to stay in balance and save time.

The flag race is the gymkhana version of tent pegging.

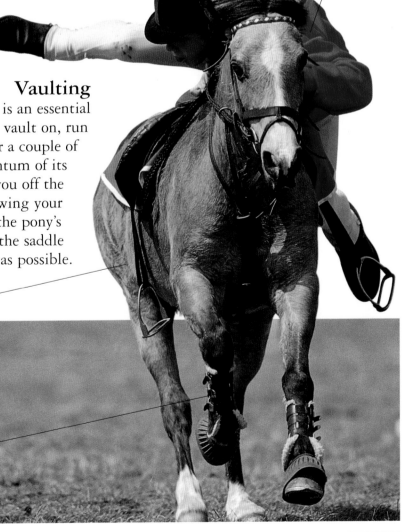

Long sleeves protect rider's arms from scrapes in case of fall.

Vaulting

Mounting a moving pony is an essential skill for gymkhanas. To vault on, run alongside the pony for a couple of strides and use the momentum of its movement to help push you off the ground as you jump. Swing your right leg well clear of the pony's hindquarters and land in the saddle as lightly as possible.

To vault, practice running alongside your pony with the stirrups flapping. Keep feet clear of irons until mounted.

This pony wears protective galloping and bell boots.

SHOWING

WHATEVER TYPE OF horse or pony you ride, you can enjoy showing. There are classes for different breeds, types, and even colors. Some classes are judged on the horse's conformation, movement, and performance in the ring; others assess the rider's ability. There are also in-hand classes, in which the horse is led rather than ridden. Horses must always be beautifully groomed.

Ridden classes

Show horses must be trained and well behaved. In some classes you will be asked to give an individual performance in front of the judge. This means riding your horse to show that it is is obedient in all its paces. Sometimes the judge will ride each horse before deciding on final placings. You may be asked to trot your horse in-hand to show off its movement.

Showing sidesaddle

Sidesaddle classes are judged on either the rider's ability or the horse's conformation and suitability to be ridden sidesaddle. The rider's outfit is called a habit, which consists of a jacket and an apron worn over breeches and boots.

Rider must sit straight and look ahead, not tilt to one side.

The judge may ask you to ride particular exercises, such as a figure eight.

Standing in a line takes practice. Your horse must be able to stand quietly and to walk away from others when asked.

Riders should wear a black, blue, or tweed jacket.

In-hand showing

There are classes for all types of horses and ponies, including young ones, and for different types and breeds. The judge assesses a horse's conformation, so you and your horse must be able to stand still, as well as walk and trot willingly without pulling or hanging back. Your horse must also be well behaved with others.

The handler should look neat and be able to control a horse. A hat, jacket, shirt and tie, and beige trousers should be worn.

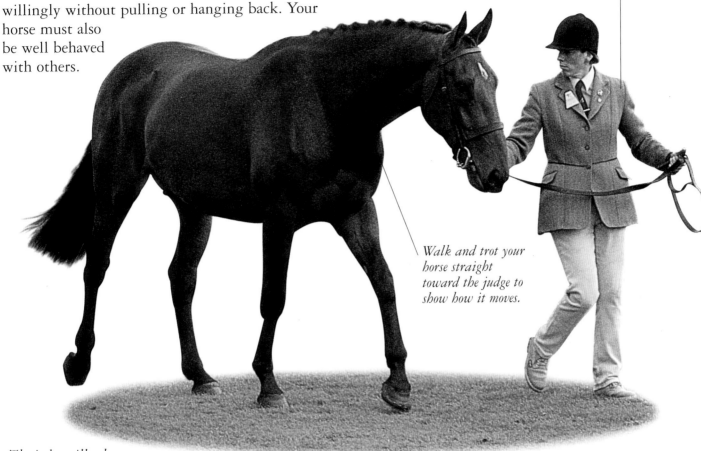

Walk and trot your horse straight toward the judge to show how it moves.

The judge will ask riders to perform some exercises.

Riding without stirrups shows the rider's balance.

Equitation classes

If you cannot find a suitable show class for your horse, you can have fun in equitation classes. These are judged on the rider's ability, not on the horse's looks. You will be asked to ride different exercises, such as figure eights and riding without stirrups. Competitors may be asked to ride each other's ponies as well as their own.

SHOWING

- The pony and its tack must be spotlessly clean

- Find out if your horse should be shown with a braided mane. Some breeds, such as Appaloosas, are not braided

- Measure your horse, as some classes specify maximum heights for horses and ponies

- Good manners and training are as important as good conformation

DRESSAGE

THERE ARE DRESSAGE TESTS for horses and riders at all stages of training. Tests comprise a series of movements designed to show that the horse is obedient and that the rider uses the correct aids. Beginner level tests include simple movements, such as circles.

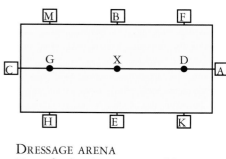

DRESSAGE ARENA
Tests for beginners are ridden in an arena measuring 130 x 66 ft (40 x 20 m). Letters around the arena indicate where a rider should start different dressage movements.

DRESSAGE MOVEMENTS

20-METER CIRCLE Dressage tests for beginners include the 20-meter circle, which is ridden in trot or canter. The circle can start from A, C, B, or E. Marks are deducted if the circles are squashed or egg-shaped, so ride in a true circle.	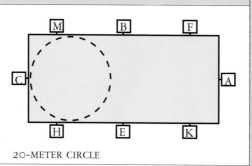 20-METER CIRCLE
DOWN CENTER LINE Tests always start and finish by riding down the center line. Be positive as you ride down the line and look where you are going, so that you are able to guide your horse in a straight line.	DOWN CENTER LINE
SERPENTINE LOOPS A three-loop serpentine is one of the most difficult movements in beginner tests. The loops must be equal in size and the rider should ride straight across the center line before starting another loop.	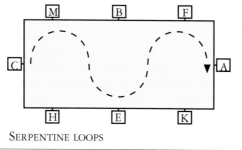 SERPENTINE LOOPS
SHALLOW LOOPS Loops of 10 ft (3 m) or 16 ft (5 m) are ridden down the long side of the arena, between the two outside markers, H and K, or F and M. While riding the loop, horse and rider should maintain a steady rhythm.	SHALLOW LOOPS

Turnout

A dressage rider and horse should be clean, tidy, and neat. At beginner level, riders wear either a tweed jacket with a shirt and tie, or a black jacket and stock. Jodhpurs can be beige or white, and boots can be long or short.

Tails can be pulled or braided. Pulled tails need bandaging to keep them in shape.

Rider creates energy using leg aids, but controls the pace using weight and hands, without pulling back.

Collected paces

At advanced levels of dressage, horse and rider are asked to work in collected paces. When a horse is collected, it is similar to a coiled spring, full of controlled energy. The horse's steps are shorter and higher than in other paces and its hind legs come farther under its body. The rider sits tall and light in the saddle to present an elegant picture.

A braided mane looks neat and helps create a good impression.

CORRECT EQUIPMENT

Riders can carry whips and wear spurs in dressage tests but must not misuse them. Martingales are not allowed but neckstraps, breastplates, and breastgirths are. Only certain bits and nosebands are allowed.

Snaffle bridles are used at beginner level.

Rider's legs create energy to lengthen stride without increasing speed.

Dressage riders should check a dressage rule book to make sure clothes and tack comply with their level of competition. Using the wrong tack will result in elimination.

Hooves are oiled for competition.

Extended paces

In extended paces, the horse's stride should be as long as possible. It is important that the horse stay balanced; it should not pull or lean on the rider's hands. Beginner level tests ask for lengthened strides, which are easier to perform. This is the first step to producing the extended paces of the advanced horse.

DRESSAGE TESTS

A DRESSAGE TEST is a series of movements performed in front of judges to show that a horse is obedient and supple, and that a rider's position and use of aids are correct. Each movement in a dressage test carries up to ten marks. At the end of the competition, the judge gives the riders a sheet with marks and comments about their test. These help riders decide what they need to practice before their next competition.

Rider practices different movements.

LEARNING YOUR TEST
Some people learn tests by drawing diagrams of the movements in the correct order; others walk the test on foot. Practice the movements with your horse, but ride them in a different order. Do not ride the complete test too many times or your horse may start to anticipate what comes next.

Top-level horses often have braids fastened with white tape.

Dressage riders plan time to warm up, making sure the horse is not too fresh or too tired when it starts the test.

Concentrate on keeping the horse balanced and energetic before entering the arena.

Make sure you know the positions of the letters.

Bandages used for warming up must be removed before starting the test.

Practice movements that you and your horse are good at. If you attempt movements that you find difficult, your horse may become tense. Concentrate on building its energy and responsiveness.

Warming up
There will probably be a special area or ring for warming up at the show. Other riders will also be using the practice area, so be aware of where they are going. Start your warm-up on a loose rein so your horse stretches its muscles. You may need up to half an hour to warm up. Try to stay relaxed, so that you do not make your horse tense.

Riding the test

As you enter the arena, look up and smile. Try to keep your breathing steady to help you stay calm. Make sure your horse is moving energetically so you ride a straight line down the center without leaving the center line. If you make a mistake, keep calm – you will have lost marks for only one movement. Remember to smile and salute the judge at the end of your test.

Dressage judges look for a horse and rider that make an elegant picture together. Movements must be accurate and performed at the right place.

Advanced horses, such as this, wear double bridles. Beginner-level horses always wear snaffle bridles.

Rider's hands are sensitive and do not pull on the reins.

SHOW JUMPING

THERE ARE SHOW JUMPING competitions for ponies and horses at all levels, ranging from small local shows to international competitions. The aim of riding a course is always to have a clear round without knocking down any fences. A course is often ridden against the clock, and the fastest clear round wins. Top-level Puissance competitions test the horse's ability to jump great heights, often 6 ft 6 in (2 m) or more.

Splint boots protect the horse's legs when it is jumping.

A body protector should be worn, even when practicing.

Novice classes

Novice classes are for inexperienced horses or riders. Fences should be low and there should be no difficult turns or tricky distances between jumps. Clear round classes, in which the aim is to jump a clear round, are an ideal introduction to show jumping. Many shows allow you to attempt more than one round so that you gain extra experience.

Distances between jumps for show jumping courses are based on a horse's canter stride measuring 12 ft (3.7 m). Ask advice when measuring distances for a pony.

SEEING A STRIDE
Learning to ride a balanced, rhythmic canter can help you meet the take-off point for a fence correctly. This is called "seeing a stride." A good way to learn how to do this is to lay a course of poles on the ground and practice riding over them in a flowing rhythm.

Rider looks ahead to the next jump.

Gridwork

Gridwork helps you and your horse become confident and athletic. A grid is a row of fences spaced at the correct distance for a horse's stride. This makes it easier for the horse to find the correct take-off points. The distances are shorter for ponies than for horses. Get an expert to help set up the grid, and always have someone on the ground who can alter the distances if necessary.

Riding a grid encourages you to improve your rhythm and to ride in a straight line.

Poles are placed at set distances on the ground.

A spread fence encourages a horse to take off correctly and jump in style.

DISTANCES BETWEEN JUMPS
Distances between fences are set to allow a certain number of strides between them. At advanced level, you may need to shorten or lengthen your horse's stride to meet a fence correctly.

An in-and-out, two fences set at a distance, allows one or two nonjumping strides between a fence.

JUMPING FAULTS

- First refusal: three faults

- Second refusal: six faults

- Third refusal: elimination

- Knockdown or foot in water: four faults

- Fall of horse or rider, or both: eight faults

- Failure to go through start or finish: elimination

- Starting round before the bell: elimination

Types of jump

Fences can be uprights or spreads, and a course will have both. Courses will include rustic poles, planks, colored fillers, brush fences, walls, and gates. Advanced courses may have water jumps. Your instructor will help you introduce your horse to different types of fence so that you and your horse approach a jump confidently.

Fillers test horse's and rider's confidence and concentration. Some horses may shy away from fillers.

IN THE RING

WHEN YOU FIRST START jumping at competitions, choose courses that have slightly smaller fences than you jump at home. This gives you and your horse confidence when jumping in strange surroundings. Walk the course carefully, and allow time to warm up before you enter the ring. If you jump a clear round and have a long wait before a jump-off, ride over two or three practice fences just before your turn.

WALKING THE COURSE

Walking the course helps the rider see potential challenges in the ring, such as fences on slightly uphill or downhill approaches. Walk the track you intend to ride so you know which route to take once you are on the horse. In novice classes, distances between combination fences are usually straightforward, but in higher-level competitions distances are more complicated.

A helper adjusts the practice fence by gradually making it taller until it is competition height.

Once your horse is jumping happily, stop. Do not tire a horse before it goes into the jumping ring.

Do not jump a practice fence too many times; six to ten turns is usually enough.

Warming up

Allow about half an hour to warm up before you enter the show ring. First try to make your horse obedient and attentive, then establish a rhythmic canter. Next, jump a few upright and spread practice fences. Practice fences should be no higher than the course you are competing over. Be considerate to other riders in the practice ring.

Riding the course

Enter the jumping ring calmly and set up a balanced canter until you receive the signal to start. Approach the first fence calmly but positively. Always look up and ahead to the next fence; never look back if you hit one, as this will unbalance your horse. As you change direction for each jump, make sure your horse is on the correct lead for canter; come back to trot if necessary. Finally, jump the fences straight on, not at an angle.

KEY	LONG ROUTE ■	SHORT ROUTE ■

JUMP-OFF
Most jumping classes have a timed jump-off for all riders who go clear in the first round. At home, practice taking a shorter route without spoiling your horse's approach or balance. Making good turns saves more time than galloping between fences, and you will be less likely to hit poles.

Rider is looking up and ahead to next jump.

Rider is keeping light rein contact that does not restrict horse.

Rider is in perfect balance. She has folded forward from the hips, and her weight is absorbed through her knee and ankle joints.

CROSS-COUNTRY

JUMPING CROSS-COUNTRY fences requires courage from both horse and rider. Fences cannot be knocked down and are tackled at a faster speed than show jumps. If the rider and horse wear correct protective equipment, and if the horse is well schooled, riding cross-country can be safe and fun. Cross-country jumping can be a competition in its own right or part of a horse trial, in which riders also take part in dressage and show jumping.

Jumping technique

To be successful at riding cross-country, a rider must be able to ride fast and remain in control. The rider should maintain a rhythm with the horse's stride so that it meets fences without having to speed up and slow down each time. The rider must stay in balance with the horse even when things go wrong.

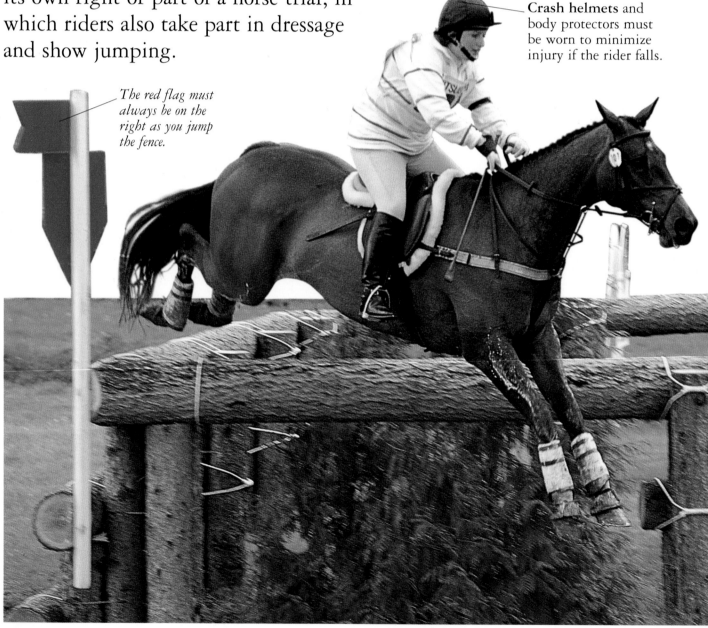

Crash helmets and body protectors must be worn to minimize injury if the rider falls.

The red flag must always be on the right as you jump the fence.

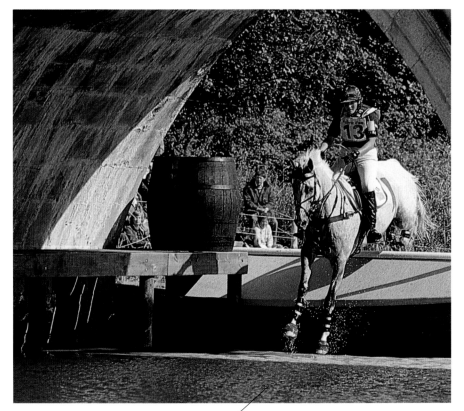

Difficult fences

Some cross-country fences are difficult and require careful riding. To tackle a water jump a horse needs power, not speed, so it does not stumble. Drop fences should be approached with energy, but more slowly than ordinary fences. To jump an in-and-out fence, the rider must be balanced, so that the horse lands over one fence and immediately takes off over another without taking a stride.

JUMPING INTO DARKNESS

Jumping into darkness, perhaps from a field into woods, is difficult for a horse. The rider should approach the fence in a straight line, so that the horse can adjust its eyesight to the changing conditions. By sitting up and riding with determination, the rider can control the horse's pace.

Landing in water slows the horse down, so a controlled approach is vital.

QUICK ROUTES

On a cross-country course, there is often a choice of routes over single fences, and over combinations with more than one jump. The quicker routes are usually more difficult and are only suitable for experienced horses and riders. If riders are unsure, they take the slower route.

Eventing

Events, or horse trials, are the most challenging of all equestrian sports. Riders have to perform a dressage test, then ride a cross-country course and a round of show jumps. Novice events are run over one day, and intermediate and advanced competitions take place over two and three days. Two- and three-day events include speed and endurance sections over a short course of steeplechase fences, and roads and tracks.

A breastplate helps prevent saddle from slipping back.

Grease on horse's legs helps it slide over fences, thus preventing serious injury.

Rider and horse must be fit.

ENDURANCE RIDING

COMPETITIVE ENDURANCE rides range from 25 miles (40 km) to more than 100 miles (160 km). There are also noncompetitive pleasure rides of about 10 miles (16 km). Arabians and part-bred Arabians are the most popular types of endurance horse at the top level, but any fit horse or pony should manage shorter distances.

Long-distance riding

Long-distance rides must be completed at set speeds, so riders have to judge the speed of their horses' trot and canter. Riders also monitor their horses' heart and respiration rates to make sure they pass the vet checks along the way.

Support team ensures that horse does not catch a chill.

SUPPORT TEAM
The support team, called the crew, is vital at top level competitive endurance riding. Each rider has a crew to meet up with at various points on a long ride. The crew cools down the horse and makes sure it is comfortable; it also provides the horse with food and water when necessary.

Sloshing down is the safest way to cool down a hot horse. Members of the support team pour water over the horse and walk it around.

Endurance horses are usually allowed to eat and drink small amounts along the ride to help maintain their energy levels.

A fit horse should not get muscle cramps.

The vet will not allow a lame or sick horse to continue.

VETERINARY CHECKS

Veterinarians check horses at "vet gates" – marked stages along the ride. The vets check that heart and respiration rates are correct and that the horse is not lame or injured. A horse that is breathing too fast is not allowed to continue until it has settled.

Horse trails

Organized rides lasting half a day or more are called treks or trail rides. Riders can take their own horse, if it is fit enough, or they can join an organized location trip. Horses need to be sure-footed and sensible, especially on rough ground or in mountainous areas. Riders who enjoy this sort of riding may go on to take part in competitive rides.

PLEASURE RIDES

Pleasure and sponsored rides are organized rides that follow a set route; some include optional jumps. These types of rides are not competitions, but riders may be asked to raise money for a charity. Pleasure rides are a good introduction to long-distance riding for young horses, since they learn to behave in unusual surroundings.

Bred for endurance

An endurance horse must have strong legs and feet, so that it can cope with long rides. The Arabian has always been a popular breed with endurance riders. It has natural stamina, speed, and agility. Although lightly built, it can carry weight. Anglo-Arabians, part-bred Arabians, and Standardbreds are also popular.

An Arabian has natural balance to cope with difficult terrain.

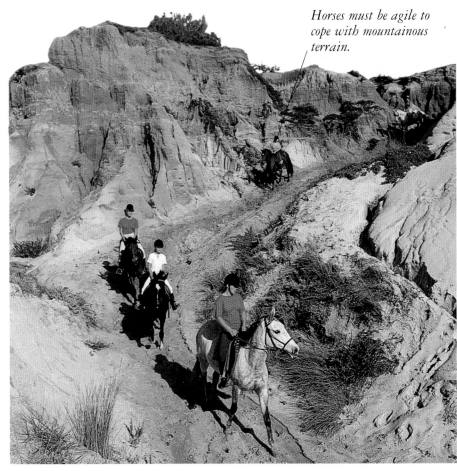

Horses must be agile to cope with mountainous terrain.

RACING SPORTS

MANY RACING SPORTS are for Thoroughbreds, but there are also special races for Quarter Horses, Arabians, and Standardbreds. Top racehorses are among the most valuable in the world; winners of the world's most prestigious races can be worth millions. Horses can be raced on the flat or over jumps. To train riding or driving horses to achieve racing speeds requires special skill and courage.

The Kentucky Derby is run on a "dirt track." This all-weather surface does not freeze.

Flat racing

Some racehorses are bred to run on the flat. They are backed as yearlings and raced as two- and three-year-olds, but often retire at an early age. Flat racehorses are handicapped by weight according to their age and past performance; this makes races more competitive. Prestigious races include the Kentucky Derby, the Breeder's Cup, and the Prix de l'Arc de Triomphe in France.

Steeplechasing

Thoroughbred steeplechasers start their racing careers when they are about four years old. The sport started in Ireland, when two riders raced between two steepled churches. Today the sport is most popular in the British Isles, but also takes place on a small scale in the U.S. and Europe. Famous races include the Grand National in the U.K. and the Pardubice in the Czech Republic.

Steeplechasers jump high, fixed fences at racing speeds over distances of up to 4.5 miles (7 km).

Riders that race on horseback are called jockeys.

Jockeys wear crash helmets covered with colored silks.

Harness racing

Standardbreds are bred to trot rather than gallop, but some reach speeds equivalent to those of galloping racehorses. Some standardbreds move their legs in diagonal pairs, like riding horses, while others pace by moving their legs in lateral pairs.

Pacers race by moving lateral legs together. The left front and hind legs move at the same time, followed by the right pair of legs.

Goggles protect a jockey's eyes from flying grass and dirt.

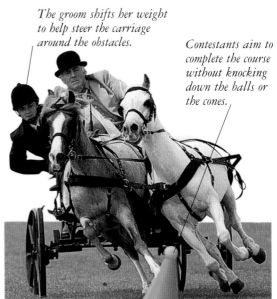

The groom shifts her weight to help steer the carriage around the obstacles.

Contestants aim to complete the course without knocking down the balls or the cones.

Competitive driving

Competitive driving combines speed with accuracy. Drivers and ponies race around a twisting course of up to 20 pairs of bollards or cones, each pair set just wide enough apart for the wheels of the carriage to pass through. Driving trials is another popular driving sport. Similar to ridden horse trials, competitors take part in three phases: dressage, the marathon, and an obstacle course.

TEAM SPORTS

TEAM SPORTS demand special skills from horse and rider. Polo is one of the oldest and most popular of sports, while polocrosse and horseball have been introduced more recently. To take part in team sports, horses and riders must be in good shape. Riders need quick reactions and good balance for making fast, sharp turns. Team sports are played on ponies and small horses.

Le Trec

Le Trec began in France about 25 years ago, and is divided into three phases. The first is orienteering, in which riders follow a map at set speeds. The second judges the control of a horse's paces. The third involves jumping, cross-country, and dismounted exercises.

The net is used to scoop and throw a soft rubber ball.

The attacking player must score as many goals as possible.

Polo

Each team has four players whose aim is to score by hitting the ball into the opposing team's goal. Player number one attacks, number four defends, while the other two hold the center. A match consists of four to six chukkas, each lasting seven minutes.

Riders can hook an opponent's stick.

Polocrosse

Polocrosse teams consist of six players. Each team is divided into two so that only three players from each are allowed on the field at a time. Player number one is the attacker and the only one who can score a goal. Player number two takes the center position, and player number three is the defender. A match is made up of six timed sections called *chukkas*, each lasting between six and eight minutes.

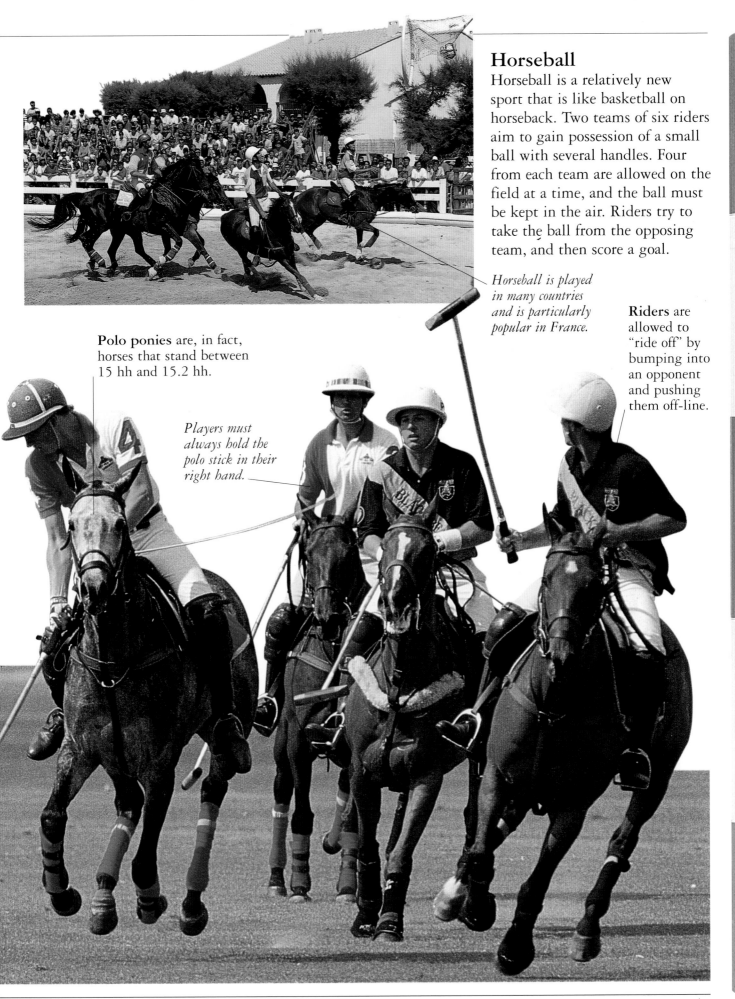

Horseball

Horseball is a relatively new sport that is like basketball on horseback. Two teams of six riders aim to gain possession of a small ball with several handles. Four from each team are allowed on the field at a time, and the ball must be kept in the air. Riders try to take the ball from the opposing team, and then score a goal.

Horseball is played in many countries and is particularly popular in France.

Riders are allowed to "ride off" by bumping into an opponent and pushing them off-line.

Polo ponies are, in fact, horses that stand between 15 hh and 15.2 hh.

Players must always hold the polo stick in their right hand.

HOMEWARD BOUND

WHEN YOU HAVE finished competing, tend to your horse. Before heading for home, cool down your horse and check for minor injuries and loose shoes. Wash any mud from its legs to uncover hidden cuts and remove shoe studs if used. Allow your horse to drink, but make sure the water is not too cold. Once back home, make sure your horse is comfortable before leaving for the day.

Care of pasture horse

At the show, cool down a pasture horse as you would any other horse. At home, check that the horse is comfortable; it should not be shivering and the base of its ears should feel warm. If necessary, stable and blanket the horse until it is dry and comfortable enough to turn out. Otherwise, turn it out so that it can walk around and roll.

Rolling helps dry off a sweaty coat and relaxes the horse.

Cooling down

Before going home, make sure your horse has cooled down so that it doesn't get a chill. Walk the horse around, with a blanket on if necessary; it may not need a blanket in hot weather. If it is hot and humid, alternate walking your horse with washing it down until the horse is comfortable.

Muscle cramping may occur if you leave your horse standing still immediately after working hard. Walk it quietly to allow it to relax, and make sure its temperature is stable.

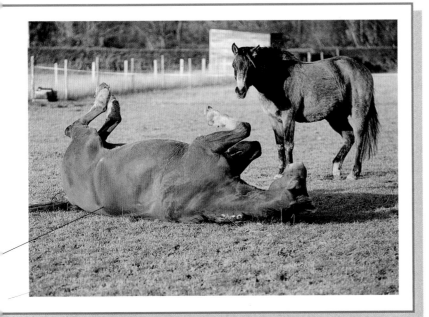

AT HOME

- Check for minor injuries and any heat or swelling in legs

- Make sure the horse has hay and water

- Provide horse with deep bed in its stall, so it can lie down

- If necessary, use extra blankets to keep horse warm

- Always make a final check before you finish for the day

- Check horse for lameness by trotting it first thing the next day

Unload with care. A tired horse may trip or stumble.

Coming home

Put a blanket on your horse to travel home. A summer sheet is necessary even in warm weather to prevent tired muscles from cramping and as protection from drafts in a moving vehicle. Offer the horse a drink before you leave the show and give it a haynet to help it relax during the journey.

In the stall

Check that your horse has traveled well and there is no sign of injury, sweating, or heat or swelling in the legs. If you are worried, get expert advice; check the horse's legs first thing the next morning. Put on stable blankets, then make sure the horse has hay and water and a clean, deep bed. If the horse is dry and relaxed, feed as normal. Before finishing for the day, check over the horse, and add or change blankets if necessary.

Give the same quantity and type of feed as normal. Clean water must be available.

SAFETY AT A SHOW

COMPETING puts extra demands on you and your horse, so it is important to make sure you both stay safe. Use the right clothes and equipment and participate in well-organized competitions only. A veterinarian and qualified first-aid experts should always be available in case of an emergency.

Special grease is smeared on the horse's legs to help it slide over cross-country fences.

Studs come in different shapes and sizes.

Splint boots help prevent injury if the horse knocks its legs together while jumping.

Bell boots protect the horse's heels.

Cross-country overgirth fastens over saddle.

Rider safety

Always ride with a hat or helmet that meets the highest safety standards. It must fit properly and the harness must always be fastened. If you are jumping, especially cross-country, wear a body protector; this helps prevent injury if you fall. Replace damaged safety equipment and do not buy these items secondhand.

Horse safety

You need to protect your horse when galloping or jumping. Boots are especially important and help prevent leg injuries. They must be the right size and fastened so that they do not slip, but are not too tight. Studs that screw into the shoes help the horse grip the ground.

Wear long-sleeved shirts to keep your arms from being scraped if you fall or ride under branches.

Wear gloves to grip slippery reins and check that the harness on the helmet is fastened securely.

Body protectors have special panels designed to absorb impact if you fall.

Correct riding boots help you keep your feet safely in the stirrup irons.

First-aid for rider

All shows should have qualified medical help available. When you arrive at a show, find out where the first-aid station is, in case you need help. If an accident occurs, try not to move an injured rider or remove the person's hat, as this may make back or neck injuries worse. Call the first-aid staff or paramedics, who will know what to do. Always try to keep calm.

Red Cross volunteers throughout the world are trained to deal with accidents.

Veterinary on call

International competitions have veterinarians in attendance. Organizers of small shows will arrange for a vet to be on call; this means that if a horse is injured, the vet can be contacted and should be there within a short time. Always take a first-aid kit so that you can deal with minor cuts and scrapes.

Always call the show vet for sudden and severe lameness.

Your horse must be protected against tetanus in case of a serious cut or injury.

Trained first-aid staff will know how to prepare an injured rider for transportation to the hospital.

SAFETY CHECKLIST

- When you get to the show, find the first-aid station

- Always make sure your helmet harness is fastened before you get on a horse

- Keep protective boots clean and in good repair. Dirty boots may cause skin problems

- Protective boots cannot be worn for showing or dressage, but you can use them when warming up

- Use studs for competition only, not when riding on the road

Glossary

There are many terms that are used specifically to describe horses, their equipment, and the way that we ride and train them. Listed below are some of the most important and frequently used ones, with a brief explanation of what they mean.

Aids Bodyweight, legs, voice, and hand signals that rider uses to communicate with horse. Martingales, whips, and spurs are considered artificial aids.

Backing Teaching a young horse or pony to accept a rider.

Bending race Mounted game in which pony and rider gallop through a row of upright poles.

Blood Used to describe a horse's breeding. A blood horse is another term for a Thoroughbred.

Bounce fences Two fences set at a distance that requires a horse to jump the first, land, then jump the second without a stride in between.

Breastplate Item of tack to help prevent saddle from slipping back. Often used for cross-country.

Browband Part of bridle that fits below ears and across top of horse's head; helps keep bridle in place.

Cannon bone The part of the foreleg between the knee and the fetlock.

Canter A three-beat gait that is faster than a trot, but slower than a gallop.

Carriage horse A term used to describe a lightly-built harness horse.

Changing the diagonal Sitting for one beat of a trot, then rising again to adjust the way a horse or pony carries the rider's weight.

Clear round jumping Jumping competition for novice horses or riders where the aim is to jump a clear round over a low course.

Cob Type of riding or driving horse with powerful neck and hindquarters, deep body, and short legs. Show cobs must be over 14.2 hh but not exceed 15.1 hh; only Welsh cobs are a breed.

Coldbloods Another term for heavy horse breeds.

Colic Abdominal pain, which must be treated as an emergency. Signs include kicking or biting at belly, sweating, and pawing ground.

Collecting ring Area at a show where competitors check in before their class. May be used as area to warm up before entering the ring.

Conformation The shape of a horse's body and legs. Good conformation means the horse is well-proportioned.

Cooler Type of rug made from absorbent fabric, which helps to dry a sweating horse.

Crew Backup team for endurance rider. It meets the horse and rider at stages along the ride to provide food, water, and any help needed.

Crossbreed A horse or pony that is the result of crossing one breed with another breed or type.

Cross surcingles Rug straps, often elasticated and made of nylon, which cross and fasten under a horse's belly to keep rugs in place.

Curry comb Metal or rubber grooming tool used for cleaning brushes. Rubber curry comb can be used to remove dried mud from horse's coat.

Dandy brush Grooming brush with stiff bristles for removing mud and loose hairs from horse's coat.

Dished head A head with a concave profile, such as the Arabian.

Double fence Two fences with one or two strides between them; distances must be correct for size of horse.

Dressage training Dressage tests are series of movements to show balance, obedience, and athletic ability of horse, and the partnership between horse and rider.

Endurance riding Sport which involves riding long distances over set course. Distances range from 25–100 miles (40–160 km).

Eventing Dressage, cross-country, and showjumping competition. Also known as horse trials.

Extended strides Action in which a horse or pony takes strides that are as long as possible, without hurrying. Can be in a walk, trot, or canter.

Farrier A person who makes and fits horseshoes.

Feral horse Horse whose ancestors were domesticated, but which now roams in the wild.

Fillers Brightly colored, solid inserts in show-jumps.

Flat racing Races without jumps for two and three-year-old Thoroughbred horses.

Fly fringe Fringe attached to horse's headcollar, which falls across the face and helps keep flies away.

Forearm The top of the foreleg down to the knee.

Freeze mark A painless security marking system where the horse is cold branded with a unique combination of letters and numbers.

Frog Sensitive V-shaped underneath part of the hoof which acts as a shock absorber.

Gait The pattern of a horse's footsteps.

Gallop A four-beat gait, the fastest pace of all.

Gamgee Padding used under leg bandages, in the stable, or when traveling.

Gelding A male horse that can no longer reproduce.

Girth The measurement around a horse's body where the girth rests.

Gridwork Gymnastic jumping exercises; jumps are set at specific distances to improve horse's athletic skill and confidence, and rider's technique.

Gymkhana Also known as mounted games; requires an athletic pony and rider.

Hacking Riding in the open, either on roads and tracks or across the open countryside.

Hand A unit of measurement to describe a horse's height at the withers. A hand is 4 in (10 cm).

Harness racing Driving races between horses harnessed to light two-wheeled vehicles called sulkies.

HH Abbreviation for hands high.

Hindquarters The back end of a horse, including the hindlegs.

Hocks Powerful joints halfway down the hindleg.

Hotblood Another term for a Thoroughbred or Arabian horse or one with a high percentage of Thoroughbred or Arabian blood.

Identichipping Form of security marking in which a tiny identichip is injected under the skin. It can be read with a scanner.

Laminitis Serious foot condition, usually linked to pony eating too much rich grass.

Lateral work Dressage and schooling exercises in which horse moves forward and sideways at the same time.

Leading leg In a canter, a horse or pony takes a longer stride with one foreleg, called the leading leg, than the other.

Lengthened strides The first stage in teaching a horse to extend its paces is to ask for strides that are longer but not faster.

Livery yard Stable yard that provides accommodation for other people's horses and ponies.

Loins The lower part of a horse's back, just in front of the quarters.

Long reining Method of training a young horse or pony to stop, start, and turn before it is ready to accept a rider.

Lunging 1. Method of training a horse or pony to accept voice commands. 2. Method where an instructor controls a horse or pony during early lessons so the novice rider can concentrate on his or her riding techniques.

Manege An enclosed area used for riding. Also called an arena or an outdoor school.

Mare A female horse more than four years old.

Martingale Piece of tack used to prevent horse from putting its head too high; main types are standing, running, and bib martingales.

New Zealand rug Waterproof rug used to keep horse warm in the field.

Noseband Part of bridle that fits across horse's face and fastens above or below the bit, depending on design. Main types include drop, cavesson, Flash, and Grakle.

Over-reach boots Protective boots to help prevent injury if a horse strikes the heel of a front foot with the toe of a back one.

Pasterns The portion of a horse's leg between the fetlock and the hoof.

Pleasure rides Noncompetitive rides over distances usually between 10–20 miles (16–32 km).

Points The external parts of a horse that make up its conformation. Also used to describe the tips of the ears, mane, tail, and lower legs.

Poll guard Fastens to headcollar and fits over the poll (top of the horse's head) to protect it when traveling.

Pulling Thinning and shaping horse's mane or tail by pulling out a few hairs at a time.

Quarter marks Designs made with a brush on a show horse's quarters.

Rein back Dressage and schooling exercise in which horse steps backward. The legs move in diagonal pairs.

Rising trot Where the rider is alternately pushed out of the saddle by a horse's or pony's movement for one beat, then sits for the next.

Serpentine Dressage and schooling exercise in which the aim is to ride loops of equal size and shape – usually three – across the arena.

Showing Classes to show horse's conformation, movement, and manners. Can be ridden or in-hand.

Side reins Reins used to control a horse's or pony's head carriage while it is being lunged.

Stallion A male horse that is used for breeding.

Steeplechasing Races for Thoroughbred horses over brush fences and ditches.

Tack Collective word for saddles, bridles, and other equipment used on riding horses and ponies.

Teeth rasping A process in which sharp edges and "hooks" on horse's teeth are removed using special files by a vet or horse dentist. Teeth must be rasped at least once a year.

Throatlatch (pronounced throatlash). Part of the bridle that fastens under horse's jaw to help keep bridle in place.

Trace clip Type of clip in which hair is removed from lower part of neck and body, following the lines of the traces of a driving harness.

Trail ride or trek A name given to long outdoor rides, often lasting for half a day or a full day.

Trot A two-beat gait in which legs move in diagonal pairs. It is faster than a walk, but slower than a canter.

Trotting up An action in which horse is led at a trot on a straight line, to identify lameness or to demonstrate horse's movement.

Turn on the forehand An exercise where a horse or pony stays in one spot and moves its hindquarters around its front end (forehand).

Vaulting Jumping onto a moving pony without putting feet in the stirrups. An essential skill for mounted games.

Vetgate Compulsory halt during a competitive endurance ride where vet checks horse's soundness, pulse, and respiration.

Vetting Pre-purchase veterinary examination in which vet examines horse for soundness and suitability for a particular purpose.

Warmbloods In general, partbred Arabian or Thoroughbred horses. Specifically, there are warmblood breeds such as the Dutch warmblood that have been bred to produce ideal modern sports horses.

Weaving Stable vice in which horse moves its head from side to side.

Weaving grid V-shaped grille that fits on stable door to reduce horse's ability to weave.

Wormer Drugs in paste of granule form that should be given to horses about every six weeks to reduce number of internal worms.

INDEX

ACKNOWLEDGMENTS

Dorling Kindersley would like to thank the following people whose assistance have made the preparation of this book possible:

CAM Equestrian Ltd, Eardisley, Hereford, for providing images of jumping poles; Lethers, Merstham, Surrey for the loan of equipment and tack. Jackki Garnham and staff, Beechwood Riding School, Woldingham, Surrey; Sandra Waylett, Gatton Park Livery, Reigate, Surrey; Ebbisham Farm Livery Stables, Walton on the Hill, Surrey, for use of their facilities. The show organizers and competitors at Chelsham Riding Club Horse Show, Farleigh, Surrey. The models Holly Clarke, Rosie Eustace, Emma de la Mothe, Kerry Meade, Alison Forrest, and Samantha Wilkinson.

Also thanks to the horses and ponies used in photography and their owners for loaning them. These are: *Cinnamon Dust* (owned by Holly Clarke); *Eliza Doolittle* and *Ginger Pick* (owned by Sandra Waylett); *Peeping Tom* (owned by Maggie Crowley); *Blondie, Tikki, Dillion, Meliton Bay* and *Garochead April* (owned by Jakki Garnham); *Face the Music* (in care of Carolyn Henderson); *Sparkie* (owned by Kerry Meade).

The publishers would also like to thank Ann Barrett for the index and Sarah Goulding for editorial assistance.

The author wishes to acknowledge Elwyn Hartley Edwards for his extensive knowledge of horse and pony breeds.

Picture Credits
The publishers would like to thank the following people for their kind permission to reproduce their photographs:

key: b bottom, c center, l left, t top, r right

Animal Photography/Sally Anne Thompson: 97br; 103tr;

Bridgeman Art Library, London & N.Y/Roy Miles Gallery, London: 88t (Sir Edwin Landseer, Arab Stallion); **J. Allan Cash Ltd:** 106t; **Bruce Coleman Ltd:** 112bc; **Richard Connor/Glen Tanar Equestrian Centre:** 148t; **John Henderson:** 153t; **Kit Houghton:** 4; 6t; 7; 35tr; 36t; 38b; 45t; 51t; 78; 86-87; 90t; 110br; 111tl; 109tr; 128b; 131b; 142; 143b; 145b; 146t; 149t, b; 153b; **Bob Langrish:** 26t; 30t; 31t; 35tl; 36bl; 59tr; 64t; 75t, br; 91t; 100br; 102t; 105tr; 108t; 109br; 112t; 113t, br; 116; 118-119; 130b; 131t; 136b; 137b; 140b; 132t; 133t; 141; 143t; 144t, b; 145tl; 146b; 147t, b; 148b; 148-149; **Pictor International:** 33tl; 86t; 111br; **Rex Features:** 60t; **Frank Spooner Pictures:** 89t (Gamma, Alain Benainous); **Tony Stone Images:** 36br.

Additional photography:
Geoff Brightling: 32tr, tl; 32-33; 33br, tl; **Andy Crawford:** 74tr; **Peter Chadwick:** 48 bl; **Kit Houghton:** 15tl, tc; 17tl, tc, tr; 21cl, cc, cr; **Bob Langrish:** 26b; 27tl, tr, br; 45t; 24l; 24-25; 25r; tc, tr; 43cl, c; 49tl; 55tl; 56bl, br; 57bl, bc; 60-61; 65cr; 70bl; 121t, c, b; 122t; **Ray Moller:** 51br; 60tr; **Stephen Oliver:** 45c; **Tim Ridley:** 27bl; 57t; 67tr; 77tr; 121c, 123.
Other photography was taken by: Philip Dowell, Mary Evans, Colin Keates, Karl Shone, Jerry Young, Berwick Woodcuts.

With thanks to all the additional horses and ponies we photographed, and their owners. These are as follows:

Page 42–43: Hippolyte, Haras National de Pau; Montemere O'Nora, Nan Thurman; Oaten Mainbrace, Mr. & Mrs. Dimmock; Hitman, Boyd Catrell; Foniks, Poul Elmerkjaer.

Page 80–81: Taws Little Buck, Kentucky Horse Park; Fruich of Dykes, Countess of Swindon; Fakir Bola, Moscow Hippodrome, Russia; Murrayton Delphinlis, June Freeman, Murrayton Stud, UK; Hopstone Shabdiz, Mrs. Scott, Henden Caspian Stud, UK.

Page 82–83: Hitman, Boyd Cantrell, Kentucky Horse Park, US.

Page 86–87: Brutt, Robert Oliver, UK; Superted, Robert Oliver, UK; Hobo, Robert Oliver, UK; Amoco Park, Spruce Meadows, Canada (also p92–93).

Page 92–93: Rambling Willie, Farrington Stables & the estate of Paul Siebert; Kentucky Horse Park, US.

Page 94–95: Barlin, Moscow Agricultural Academy, Russia; Chatsworth Belle; Mrs. Hampton, Briar Stud, UK; Fruich of Dykes, Countess of Swinton; Allendale Vampire; Miss M Houlden, Havenstud, UK; Waverhead – William, Mr. & Mrs. Errington, UK.

Page 96–97: Tressor des Pins, Haras de Pall, France; Ausdan Svejk, John Goddard Fenwick & Lyn Moran, Dyfed, UK; Orchidea, Sadamo Tombini, Perego, Italy.

Page 98–99: Hopstone Shabdiz, Mrs. Scott, Henden Caspian Stud, UK; Pegasus of Kilverstone, Lady Fischer, Kilverstone Wildlife Park, UK; Meriam Beluna, Peltia Jaya Stable, Jakarta, Indonesia; Mels Lucky Boy, Mr. D Stewart, Kentucky Horse Park, US.

Page 100–101: Edison, Mrs. Dejonge; Soir d'Avril, Haras Nationaux de l'Isle de Lion d'Angers.

Page 102–103: Miss Mill, Mr. R. J. Lampard; Oaten Mainbrace, Mr. & Mrs. Dimmock, UK.

Page 104–105: Tango, Haras National de Saint Lo, France; Roy; Kentucky Horse Park, US.

Page 106–107: Golden Nugget, Sally Chaplin, UK; Laurel Keepsake II, P. Adams and Sons, Laurel Farm, UK.

Page 108–109: Leikner, Kentucky Horse Park, US; Delights Moondus, Andrew and Jane Shan, Kentucky Horse Park, US.

Page 110–111: Mr. Starpasser, Pat Butcher, Canada; Redounet, Mr. Contreras, Les Saintes Maries de la Mer, France.

USEFUL ADDRESSES

Here are the addresses of some associations and other organizations that can help you find out more about horse and pony breeds and riding clubs in your area:

American Association of Horsemanship Safety Inc.
P.O. Drawer 39
Fentress, TX 78622-0039
Tel: (512) 488-2128
Fax: (512) 488-2319

American Endurance Ride Conference
701 High Street, #203
Auburn, CA 95603
Website: www.aerc.org

American Horse Shows Association
220 East 42nd Street
New York, NY 10017
Tel: (212) 972-2172
Fax: (212) 983-7286
Website: www.ahsa.org

The American Polocrosse Association
PO Box 853
Johnson City, TX 78636
Website:
www.ILSweb.net/polocrosse/

American Riding Instructor Association
P.O. Box 282
Alton Bay, NH 03810
Tel: (603) 875-4000
Fax: (603) 875-7771

American Youth Horse Council Inc.
4903 Iron Works Pike
Lexington, KY 40511
Tel: (800) TRY AYHC
Fax: (606) 299-9849

Australian Equine Veterinary Association
PO Box 371
Artarmon
NSW 2064,
Australia
Tel: (02) 9411 2733

CHA/Association for Horsemanship Safety and Education
P.O. Box 188
Lawrence, MI 49064
Tel: (616) 674-8074

Equestrian Federation of Australia
196 Greenhill Road
Eastwood
SA 5063,
Australia
Tel: (08) 8357 0077

Equestrian Federation Saddle Horse Council
70 Falters Road
Wilberforce
NSW 2756,
Australia
Tel: (02) 4575 1341

Horsemanship Safety Association Inc.
517 Bear Road
Lake Placid, FL 33852
Tel: (941) 465-0289
Fax: (800) 798-8106
E-mail: HSANews@aol.com

North American Riding for the Handicapped Association
P.O. Box 33150
Denver, CO 80233
Tel: (303) 452-1212

Pony Club Association of NSW
PO Box 980
Glebe
NSW 2037,
Australia
Tel: (02) 9552 2800

United States Combined Training Association
525 Old Waterford Rd., NW
Leesburg, VA 20176
Website: www.eventingusa.com

United States Dressage Federation
P.O. Box 6669
Lincoln, NE 68506-0669
Website: www.usdf.org

United States Equestrian Team
(and Olympic Training Center)
Pottersville Road
Gladstone, NJ 07934
Website: www.uset.com

United States Pony Club
4071 Iron Works Pike
Lexington, KY 40511
Tel: (606) 254-7669
Fax: (606) 233-4652
Website: www.ponyclub.org